101 Needlepoint Stitches
and How to Use Them

Fully Illustrated with Photographs
and Diagrams

by

Hope Hanley

Dover Publications, Inc., New York

Published in Canada by General Publishing Company, Ltd., 30 Lesmill Road, Don Mills, Toronto, Ontario.
Published in the United Kingdom by Constable and Company, Ltd., 10 Orange Street, London WC2H 7EG.

This Dover edition, first published in 1986, is an unabridged and corrected republication of the work originally published by Charles Scribner's Sons, New York, in 1977 under the title *The Craft of Needlepoint: 101 Stitches and How to Use Them*. That work was based on *Needlepoint*, originally published by Charles Scribner's Sons, New York, in 1964, and revised and enlarged in 1975.

Manufactured in the United States of America
Dover Publications, Inc., 31 East 2nd Street, Mineola, N.Y. 11501

Library of Congress Cataloging in Publication Data

Hanley, Hope.
    101 needlepoint stitches and how to use them.

    Reprint. Originally published: The craft of needlepoint. New York : Scribner, 1977.
    Includes index.
    1. Canvas embroidery.   I. Title.   II. Title: One hundred one needlepoint stitches and how to use them.   III. Title: One hundred and one needle point stitches and how to use them.
TT778.C3H359   1986   746.44′2   85-20743
ISBN 0-486-25031-8

THE STITCHES

The most efficient way to learn the stitches is to do them. Then you can see just how they will look for your design purposes. A picture or diagram just does not show the size relative to other stitches or the contrasting textures. Working a sampler is really an excellent way to make these discoveries. It is also a permanent record of the stitches that you are not liable to give away as you would with finished items. All you need to make a sampler is half a yard or less of mono-canvas, less than that of a two-thread canvas, needles and about four ounces of yarn. Bind the edges of the canvas with binding tape or masking tape and you are all set to go. A dressmakers' chalk will mark off squares if you want to make a precise sampler, or you can just mix them random style. You will find as you work that design ideas will suggest themselves to you, so write them down; you'll surely forget them otherwise. A sampler will show you just which stitches are the wool-eaters, and which bias the canvas. Keep in mind when you choose your sampler wool that light colors show texture best.

Two of the following stitches have tramé as a base. It might be well to explain now just what it is. Some canvases are sold with the background and possibly the subject done in a long horizontal basting-like stitch. This is tramé. It is used on these canvases to show what colors to use and to indicate the design. The right amount of wool and the right colors of wool are included with this type of canvas as a sort of kit. One stitches right over the tramé as though it were not even there. It is an understitching. It must be laid on in irregular series, as it will form ridges if done in regular rows. Tramé may also be used to add body to a stitch, to beef it up, and this is its purpose with the stitches included here. To figure the extra wool needed to tramé, just halve the number of mesh per inch of the canvas you are using and add two inches to the figure for each square inch. Thus if you are using fourteen mesh canvas, half of fourteen is seven plus the two added inches equals nine extra inches of wool for each square inch of tramé.

The following table lists suggested uses for the stitches. It is just a guide line for you to follow until you are familiar enough with the stitches to make your own judgments on them. The word filling means a stitch to be used in an enclosed area, not the background.

Only stitches which adequately cover the canvas have been included in the following collection. In tapestry no warp threads are allowed to show through, so why let canvas show through in needlepoint? No stitch combinations have been included, just the fundamental stitch. Think up your own combinations, as there are literally hundreds of them.

Tramé on penelope canvas

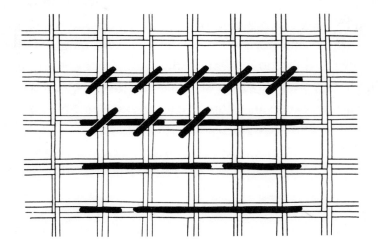

From the number of initials on the motif sampler it would appear that a group of friends all took part in making it. Many colors were used in the figures, the background is black, and the stitch is the half cross. *The Smithsonian Institution, Washington, D.C.*

6

	filling	back-ground	grounding, striking pattern by itself	detail, single specimen	slow to work up	quick to work up	best on mono-canvas	best on two-thread canvas
Rep Stitch	×				×			×
Feather Half Cross Stitch	×		×			×	×	×
Cross Stitch	×	×			×			×
Cross Stitch Tramé	×				×			×
Oblong Cross Stitch	×					×		×
Bargello Cross Stitch		×	×			×		×
Oblong Cross Stitch with Back Stitch	×				×			×
Upright Cross Stitch	×	×				×	×	
Smyrna Cross Stitch	×		×	×	×		×	×
Double Cross Stitch	×					×	×	
Double Stitch	×	×	×			×		×
Rice Stitch	×			×	×			×
Oblong Rice Stitch	×				×			×
Double Straight Cross Stitch	×		×			×	×	
Double Leviathan Stitch	×		×	×	×		×	×
Greek Stitch	×			×		×	×	×
Long Armed Cross Stitch	×			×		×	×	×
Diagonal Long Armed Cross Stitch	×				×		×	×
Closed Cat Stitch			×			×	×	×
Running Cross Stitch				×	×			×
Tied-Down Cross Stitch	×		×	×		×	×	×
Woven Cross Stitch Square			×	×	×		×	×
Woven Cross Stitch			×		×		×	×

	filling	back-ground	grounding, striking pattern by itself	detail, single specimen	slow to work up	quick to work up	best on mono-canvas	best on two-thread canvas
Fancy Cross Stitch			×	×		×	×	×
Triple Cross Stitch				×		×	×	
Sprat Stitch			×	×	×		×	×
Button Stitch			×	×	×		×	×
Montenegrin Cross Stitch	×			×		×	×	×
Encroaching Long Cross Stitch	×	×	×			×	×	×
Check Stitch			×			×	×	
Diagonal French Stitch	×		×			×	×	
Herringbone Stitch	×		×		×			×
Reverse Herringbone Stitch	×		×		×			×
Diagonal Reverse Herringbone Stitch	×		×		×			×
Two-Color Herringbone Stitch			×			×		×
Plaited Gobelin Stitch			×			×		×
Bazar Stitch			×		×			×
Velvet Stitch	×				×			×
Fern Stitch	×					×	×	×
Long and Short Oblique Stitch			×			×		×
Point de Tresse Stitch			×	×	×		×	×
French Stitch	×		×		×			×
Knotted Stitch	×				×		×	×
Rococo Stitch	×		×	×	×		×	×
Diagonal Shell Stitch			×		×		×	
Roumanian Stitch	×					×	×	
Gobelin Stitch	×	×				×	×	

	filling	back-ground	grounding, striking pattern by itself	detail, single specimen	slow to work up	quick to work up	best on mono-canvas	best on two-thread canvas
Renaissance Stitch	×				×			×
Gobelin Tramé Stitch	×		×			×		×
Brick Stitch	×	×				×	×	
Irish Stitch		×	×			×	×	
Bargello		×	×			×	×	
Old Florentine Stitch			×			×	×	
Parisian Embroidery Stitch	×	×	×			×	×	
Hungarian Embroidery Stitch	×	×	×̃			×	×	
Shaded Stripe Stitch	×		×			×	×	
Enlarged Parisian Embroidery Stitch			×			×	×	
Slanting Gobelin Stitch	×	×				×	×	×
Wicker Stitch	×		×			×	×	
Diagonal Wicker Stitch	×		×		×		×	×
Interlocking Gobelin Stitch	×				×		×	×
Encroaching Oblique Stitch	×	×				×	×	×
Oblique Slav Stitch	×					×	×	×
Kalem Stitch or Knit Stitch	×	×				×	×	×
Diagonal Knit Stitch	×	×				×	×	×
Mosaic Stitch	×	×	×			×	×	×
Mosaic Stitch Done Diagonally	×	×	×			×	×	×
Scotch Stitch	×		×			×	×	×
Checker Stitch		×	×			×	×	×
Point Russe Stitch				×		×	×	×
Scotch Stitch Worked Diagonally		×	×			×	×	×
Moorish Stitch		×	×			×	×	×
Cashmere Stitch	×	×	×			×	×	×

	filling	back-ground	grounding, striking pattern by itself	detail, single specimen	slow to work up	quick to work up	best on mono-canvas	best on two-thread canvas
Cashmere Stitch Worked Diagonally	×	×	×			×	×	×
Brick Cashmere Stitch	×	×	×			×	×	×
Danish Knot Stitch	×			×	×		×	×
Milanese Stitch		×	×			×	×	×
Oriental Stitch		×	×			×	×	×
Byzantine Stitch		×	×			×	×	×
Jacquard Stitch		×	×			×	×	×
Web Stitch	×				×		×	
Stem Stitch	×		×		×		×	×
Perspective Stitch			×	×	×		×	×
Leaf Stitch	×	×	×	×		×	×	×
Star Stitch	×				×			×
Eye Stitch	×		×	×	×		×	×
Ray Stitch	×				×		×	×
Diamond Eyelet Stitch	×		×		×		×	×
Reverse Eyelet Stitch	×			×		×	×	×
Triangle Stitch			×	×		×	×	
Triple Leviathan Stitch			×	×	×		×	
Flower Stitch				×		×	×	
Surrey Stitch	×		×			×	×	×
Turkey Work	×		×			×	×	×
Raised Work Stitch	×		×			×		×
Chain Stitch	×				×			×
Laced Chain Stitch	×		×			×	×	×
Darning Stitch	×		×		×		×	

The Half Cross Stitch

The basic stitch in needlepoint or canvas work is a short slanting stitch worked over one intersection of the canvas mesh. It is called the half cross stitch because it is half of a cross stitch; a cross stitch is two slanting stitches worked in the opposite directions to each other over one intersection of the canvas mesh. There are three ways of working the half cross stitch. They all achieve the same effect on the face of the canvas; it is only on the back of the canvas that you can determine the method used. All of the half cross stitches have aliases (this goes for the fancy stitches too). To clarify this situation the most popular name is given first with the other names following.

Quick Point

Quick point is the simplest of the half cross stitches. It is nothing more than a whip stitch done on canvas. It biases the canvas quite badly, which is its chief fault; a lesser fault is that it cannot be worked on mono-canvas. Try it and you will see, the wool slides about without the two-thread weave to hold it firmly in place.

It is worked from left to right; when one row is done, turn the canvas upside down and start the next row. It is simple enough for small children to learn and has the added advantage for them of allowing them to work from bottom to top if they prefer. When they are older they can be taught the basket weave.

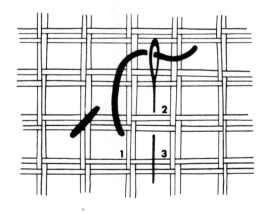

Needlepoint terminology varies somewhat from book to book. Frequently you will find the term "tent stitch" used to refer to any short slanting stitch worked over one intersection of the canvas mesh, with the term "half cross stitch" used exclusively for the quick point stitch.

The Continental Stitch or Tent Stitch

The continental stitch is shown next because one uses it in working the basket weave stitch. This stitch is best used for working small details and single vertical or horizontal lines of stitches. The reason it is not used for large areas is that it biases the canvas quite badly. You will find that stitches that slant both on the face and the back of the canvas usually are biasers; the canvas is more or less tied into a slanted position. Working the continental stitch in a frame will correct the bias.

The continental stitch is worked from right to left, then the canvas is turned upside down to work the next row. With the continental stitch, the needle slants diagonally under two canvas threads; as you complete one stitch you are setting yourself up for the next stitch. It works well on all of the canvases.

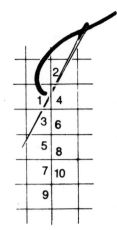

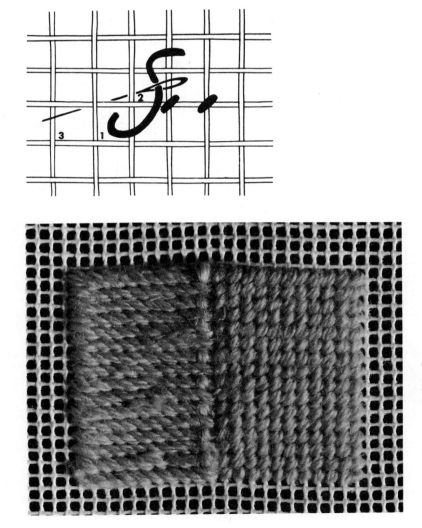

The continental stitch, the front on the right, the back on the left

The Basket Weave Stitch or Bias Tent Stitch or the Diagonal Stitch

The basket weave stitch is the preferred half cross stitch. It should be used whenever possible, for subject matter as well as backgrounds. Its great virtue is that it does not bias the canvas. It is also easier to work in that one does not have to keep turning the canvas around and around. The importance of preventing bias is to minimize the amount of blocking the canvas will need at completion. A badly biased canvas may take more than one blocking to straighten it out and may never block completely straight. Try to use the basket weave as much as possible, keeping the use of the continental to a minimum. The basket weave has a firm backing which looks as if it had been woven, hence its name. It can be worked on all canvases.

The needle passes under two canvas threads for each stitch, horizontally on an up row, and vertically on a down row. A continental-like stitch at the end of each row will help you finish your present row and start you off on the next row.

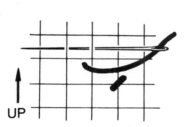

Needle always goes under two mesh horizontally on 'up' row.

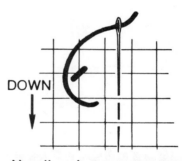

Needle always goes under two mesh vertically on 'down' row.

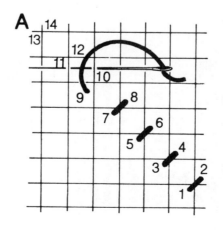

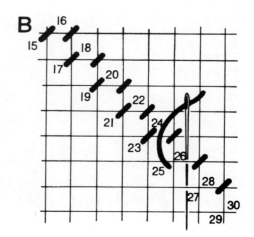

There is a unique way to finish off your thread with the basket weave stitch that will prevent those unsightly ridges that one sees when the light falls on the canvas wrong. On your last stitch simply take your needle through to the back of the canvas and then bring it out about an inch from where you went in. Leave a little tag of wool hanging on the face of the canvas. As you work subsequent rows, you will slowly cover up the wool left on the back of the canvas; pull the tag on the face through to the back when you reach it. Looking at the back of your work it will be very difficult to see where a thread started or finished.

If you must leave your work at the end of a row and you can't remember whether you are on a down or up row, look on the back of the canvas to see if the last row left vertical or horizontal stitches on the back. If horizontal, then you know your next row is a down row, if vertical, the next row is an up row. This is important, because if you work two consecutive rows in the same direction an odd high line of stitches is the result.

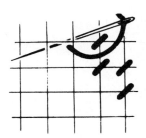

Continental stitch at end of 'up' row ends that row and begins the next.

Vertical continental stitch finishes 'down' row and starts the next row.

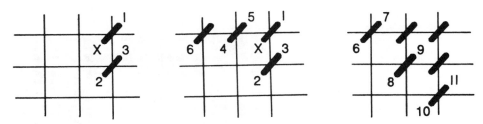

How to start the basket weave stitch in a corner

The basket weave stitch, the front on the right, the back on the left

The Rep Stitch or the Aubusson Stitch

This stitch is really a variation of the quick point stitch. It can be worked only on a two-thread or penelope canvas, then it is stitched over both warp threads and only one of the weft. The result has the look of rep silk. It does bias the canvas.

The Feather Half Cross Stitch

This stitch may be worked in rows just by itself or alternating with rows of half cross stitch. It makes a hard-textured stripe. There is little more wool on the back of the canvas than with the quick point version of the half cross stitch. This is one of the reasons they go together so well. Each stitch must be eased into place to make an even line of stitches and to close the knot so that the canvas won't peek through. It helps if you hold the working wool down with the thumb of your non-needle-wielding hand as you ease into the knot. If you plan to work solid rows of just the feather half cross stitch work from the left of the canvas to the right.

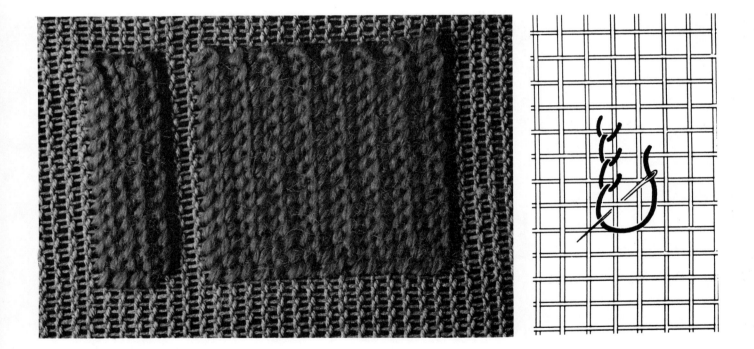

The Cross Stitch

The cross stitch was much used by our ancestors for their pictorial needlepoint pictures; it was also a favorite of early English needle-pointers. The cross stitch can be worked on all canvases, though it looks best on the two-thread variety. You will need less wool in your needle than you would if you were working the half cross stitch. For instance, if you use a full strand of Persian for the half cross stitch, for the cross stitch two threads will probably suffice. Some people prefer to work a row of half cross stitch and then return, crossing the half crosses as you come, so to speak. The single trip method here dia-gramed is recommended for mono-canvas. The important thing to remember with the cross stitch is to make sure all the crosses cross in the same direction. There are several variations of this stitch, but this is the basic one.

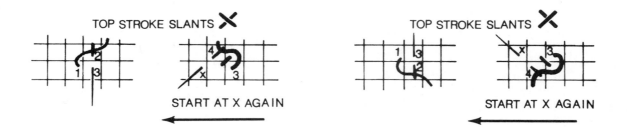

TOP STROKE SLANTS ✗   TOP STROKE SLANTS ✗

START AT X AGAIN   START AT X AGAIN

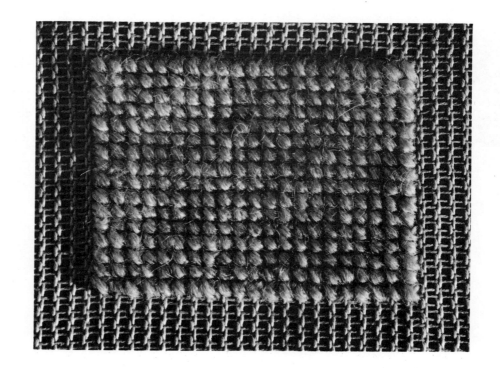

The Cross Stitch Tramé

The cross stitch from a distance looks very much like plain old half cross stitch, but a cross stitch tramé cannot be mistaken this way. It sits up on its understitching and the cross is quite obvious. It is appropriate to use when a fine texture is not required. When doing the tramé understitching do be sure that you are *not* doing it evenly. Make some of your long stitches over five warp threads, then over six and seven. It is important not to have a pattern of tramé stitches showing through the cross stitches. This cross stitch is the same as the one before except that it is done over two mesh each way. Don't forget to make all the crosses in the same direction.

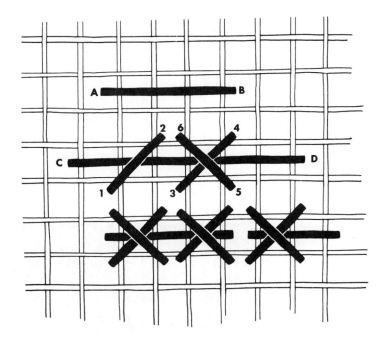

The Oblong Cross Stitch

The oblong cross stitch is a tall cross stitch which can be done on both canvases. On mono-canvas it looks a little like rope, on penelope the crosses are more obvious. It is a hard stitch to keep uniform; the crosses tend to straggle unless the tension is even on each stitch. This stitch does not provide much of a backing. Don't forget to make all the crosses in the same direction.

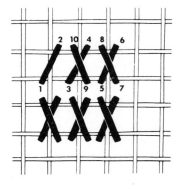

The Bargello Cross Stitch

Bargello, as you know, should be worked only on mono-canvas or a closely woven leno canvas. The bargello cross stitch enables one to work bargello patterns on two-thread or penelope canvas. The slight slant of the long cross stitch is barely discernible. The standard amount of wool used for the half cross stitch will probably suffice for this stitch too, but you will have to experiment with your canvas and your wool to find out. This is a good stitch for bargello belts. Make sure that all the stitches cross in the same direction. Again, please note, this stitch is not meant for mono-canvas.

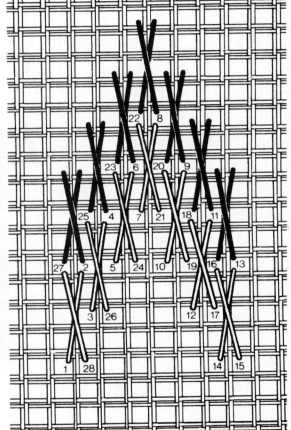

The Oblong Cross Stitch with Back Stitch

This stitch is almost the same as the previous stitch. You might call this one a tall cross stitch with a belt. If you require a very hard wearing, rough feeling stitch, here it is. It is sort of knotty looking, and is not at all apt to snag. This stitch is similar in appearance to the knotted stitch but they are constructed differently. This stitch is slow to work up, does not pull the canvas out of shape, and does have a very firm backing. Its major fault is that it is a wool-eater.

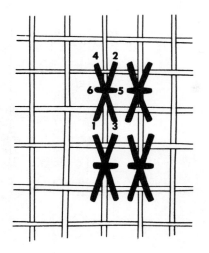

The Upright Cross Stitch

The upright cross stitch gives a pin seal leather-like look. It is a tough stitch and hard to snag. It is useful for subject as well as backgrounding. It does not bias the canvas. If the first two or three rows of this stitch don't look like much of anything, persist, and by about the sixth or seventh row it will start taking shape. Use a little less wool in your needle than you would ordinarily. If you stitch it diagonally as shown here, you will find that it works up rather quickly.

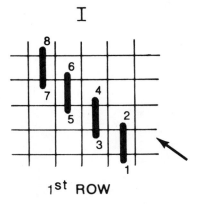

I

1st ROW

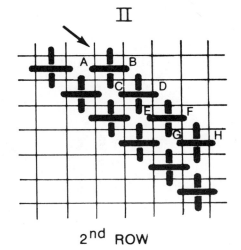

II

2nd ROW

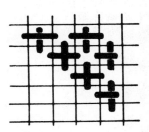

III

Fitting the stitch in a corner

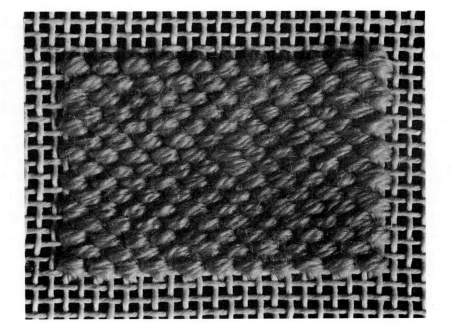

The Smyrna Cross Stitch

The Smyrna cross stitch is one of needlepoint's most versatile stitches. It is not only decorative and highly textured, but it is functional too. It can be used to join two pieces of canvas. Just place one edge of canvas over the other, matching mesh for mesh, baste them together, and then work the Smyrna cross stitch over the whole business. The bulk of the stitch neatly covers the cut edges of the top layer of canvas. Its only drawback is that you cannot work half a Smyrna cross stitch; the area in which it is used must be divisible by two both ways. Be sure all the top stitches are worked in the same direction.

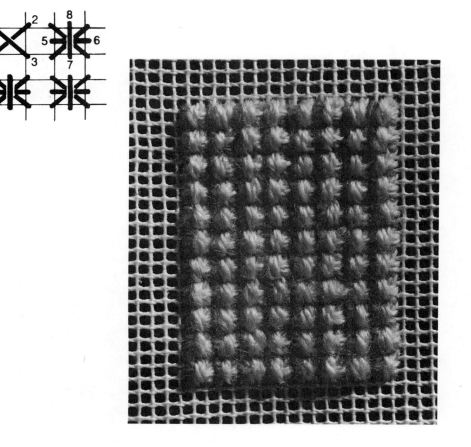

The Double Cross Stitch

The double cross stitch really could be called the two cross stitch. This would be a better description since this stitch is really a combination of the cross stitch and the upright cross stitch. The wool must fit the canvas exactly for this stitch, just fat enough, otherwise canvas will show through. The double cross stitch is attractive done in one color; it is also attractive with the cross stitch done in one color and the upright cross done in another color. Don't forget to watch the direction of your crosses.

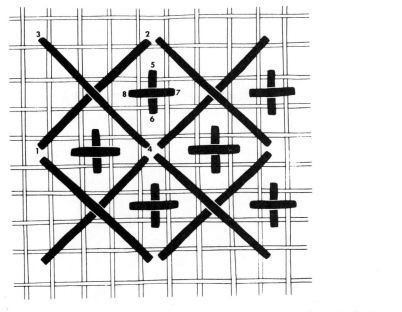

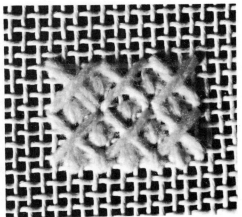

24

The Double Stitch

The double stitch is very like the double cross stitch in name and the way it is done. The big difference is that the big cross stitch is a long cross stitch. This is a difficult stitch to work on fine canvas. It is recommended that you use it on ten mesh or lower. Work the large crosses first and then fill in with the little ones. The result is a neat woven effect that is heightened if you work the little crosses in another color. Watch your cross direction.

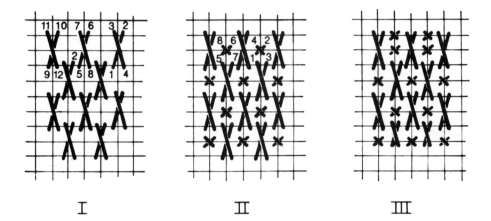

I   II   III

The Rice Stitch or the Crossed Corners Stitch or the William and Mary Stitch

The rice stitch is another one that must have the wool fitting exactly if the stitch is to be effective at all. You must experiment until you are satisfied that no canvas shows through the wool but that at the same time the stitch does not look too crowded. The rice stitch is really just the cross stitch with its arms tied down. Try doing the cross stitch in one color and the tie-downs in another shade of the same color.

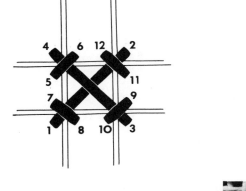
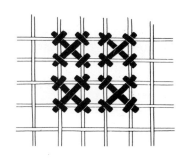

The Oblong Rice Stitch

Unless the oblong rice stitch is worked in two colors it has a pretty nondescript appearance. Use the standard amount of wool for the long cross stitch and a thread less for the tie-down stitches. Be careful the canvas does not buckle or draw up while working the long cross stitches. There will be quite a bit of wool on the back of the canvas because of all the little tie-down stitches.

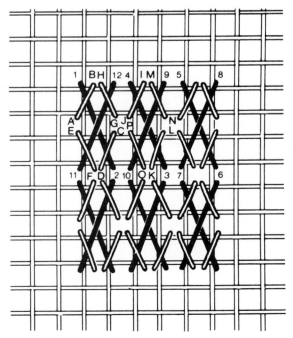

The Double Straight Cross Stitch

This stitch is very similar to the upright cross stitch. The big difference is that the double straight cross stitch must be worked over four mesh each way and it has an extra cross to hold it down. It is very important to fit the wool to the canvas just so or the canvas will show through. Make sure all of your little crosses are going in the same direction.

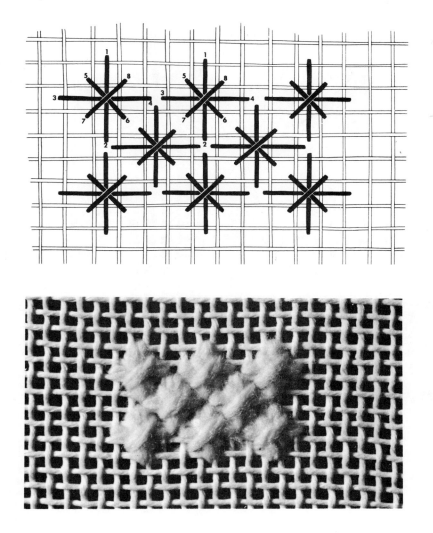

The Double Leviathan Stitch

The double leviathan stitch may be used in rows or as a separate decorative stitch. A single square of the stitch makes quite a high bump on the canvas, very much like the popcorn stitch in crochet. If necessary to cover the canvas a long upright stitch may be used between the squares of stitches. When designing the space for this stitch make sure it is divisible by four since this stitch does not halve very well.

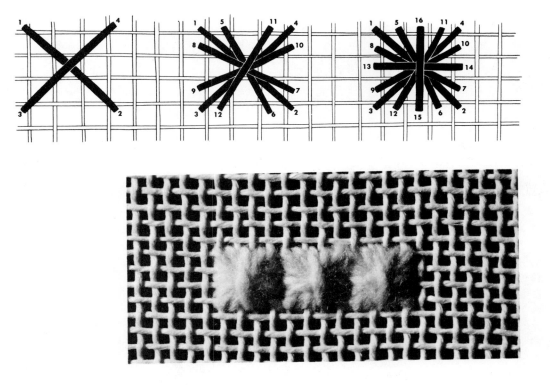

The Greek Stitch and
the Long Armed Cross Stitch

These stitches look alike from the front of the canvas; it is only from the back of the canvas that one can tell which stitch was used. The long armed cross stitch is a little clumsy to work, though the Portuguese seem to prefer it. They make a special kind of rug on a jute canvas using the stitch exclusively. These are called Arraiolos rugs. Both stitches form a thin braid, very nice for borders. If you work multiple stripes of it, they should all point in the same direction.

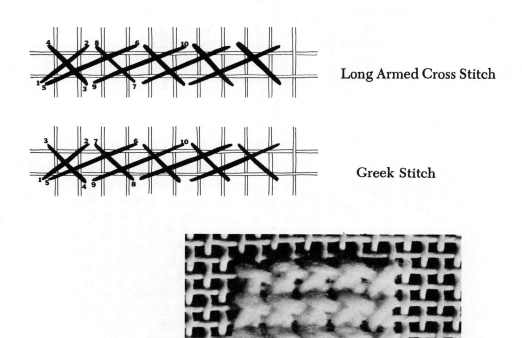

Long Armed Cross Stitch

Greek Stitch

The Diagonal Long Armed Cross Stitch

This stitch makes a nice companion to the Greek version of the previous stitch. It is a little tricky to catch on to at first, but once you have the rhythm of it you are all set. It makes a firm braid on the face of the canvas and like the previous stitch has little wool on the back. It does bias the canvas. A frame would be advisable for large areas of the stitch.

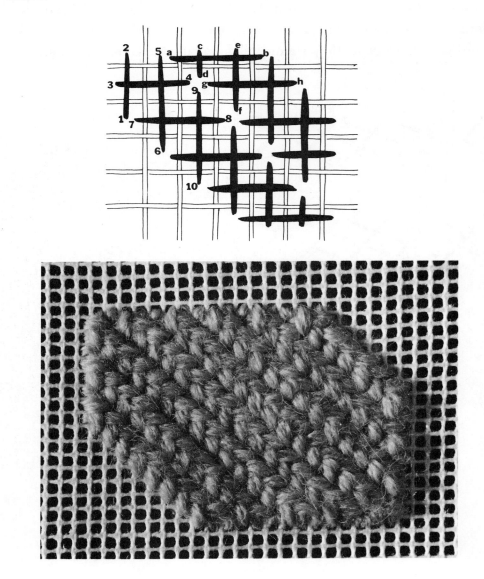

The Closed Cat Stitch or
the Telescoped Herringbone Stitch

This stitch is really just a variation of the long armed cross stitch or the herringbone stitch; compare the diagrams. It makes a tight, hard ridge-like braid; as a grounding it looks like corduroy. It may be worked over two or three mesh and it does not bias the canvas.

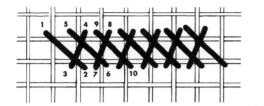

The Running Cross Stitch or the Long Cross Stitch

The running cross stitch works best on a two-thread canvas, but it is unusual in that it can be worked over just one set of mesh instead of two. It serves very well between rows of Gobelin stitch or Roumanian stitch, stitches that otherwise show canvas on their outer edges. It makes a high ridged braid and is so easy to work. If used as a single braid use the normal amount of wool; if used in multiple rows use about half the amount you usually would.

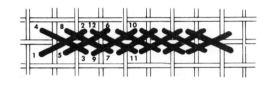

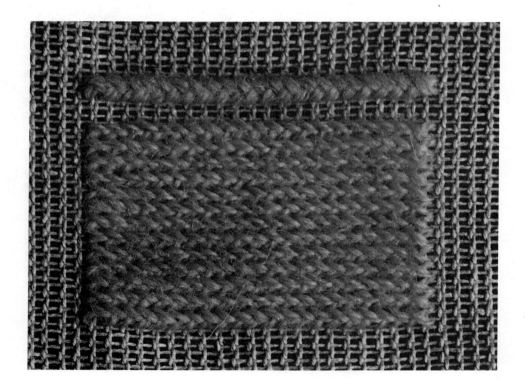

The Tied Down Cross Stitch

This stitch is a Victorian stitch that was used by itself to embellish a field of half cross stitches. It can be used as grounding, however, as shown here. You will need less wool in your needle when used as a grounding; alternating colors give it more definition. It is worked in diagonal rows. Be sure that all the top crosses cross in the same direction.

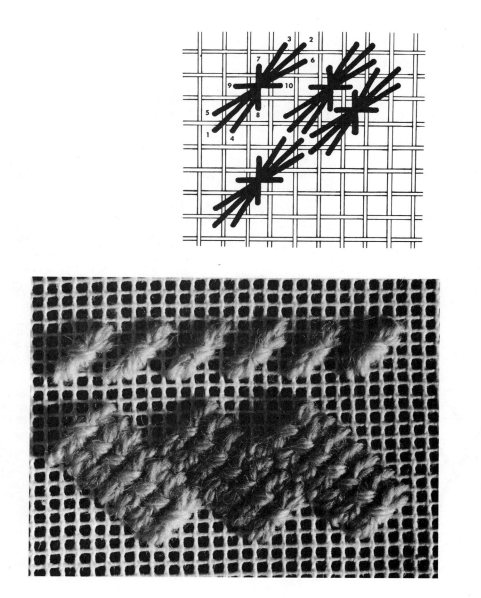

The Woven Cross Stitch Square and the Woven Cross Stitch

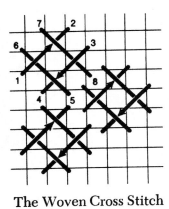

The Woven Cross Stitch
as a grounding

The woven cross stitch square version of this stitch may be worked as a specimen that is all by itself in a field of half cross stitches or as a grounding. When used as a grounding it is very attractive worked in two colors. Be sure you weave all the crosses alike. You will probably need more wool in your needle than usual to cover the canvas.

The woven cross stitch itself can also be used as a grounding but the spaces on the sides must be filled in with half cross stitches. This stitch also will need more wool to cover the canvas.

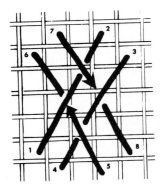

The Woven Cross Stitch Square

The Woven Cross Stitch

The Fancy Cross Stitch

This stitch is reminiscent of the double straight cross stitch and the Smyrna cross stitch. It dates from the late 19th century when stitches were apt to be big and sprawly. This one is; it makes a very busy grounding. The wool must fit the canvas just right or the canvas will show through around the largest cross stitches. Experiment until you have enough wool in your needle. Make the smaller cross stitches in another color. Make sure all your cross stitches cross in the same direction.

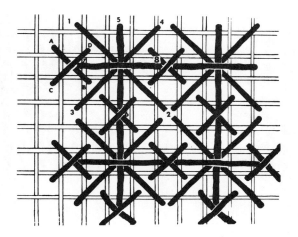

The Triple Cross Stitch

This cross stitch is just a specimen stitch and a very pretty one, too. The background of half cross stitch must be worked first because the cross stitch itself reaches out into the background. The very long strokes are worked right into the first row of half cross stitch. (See diagram.) Leave a bare spot of canvas six mesh high by two mesh wide in the form of a Greek or "red" cross. Make the cross stitch a different color than the background for the best results.

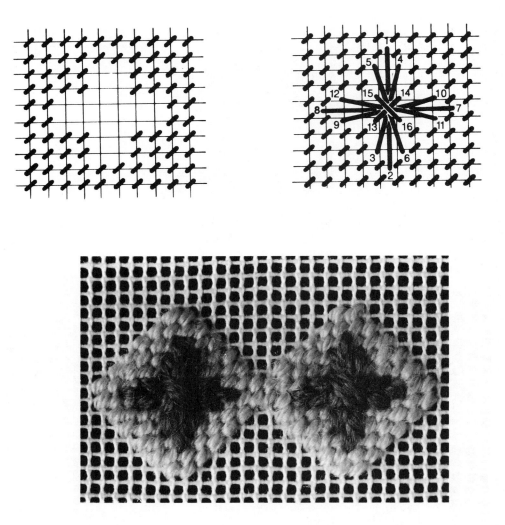

The Sprat Stitch

The name of this stitch will be familiar to seamstresses as it is a tailoring stitch adapted to needlepoint. It may be worked in one color throughout or in alternating colors. It is important that you are always consistent in stitching stroke number 5 on the left. This will ensure that the stitches cross each other the same way on every stitch. There is surprisingly not much wool on the back of the canvas, but you may need an extra thread of wool in your needle to cover the canvas. If canvas shows through between the sprats, as it will occasionally, tuck a half cross stitch over the offending mesh, using a little less wool in your needle, or back stitch a line between each sprat. The stitch can be halved in three mesh; therefore you will need a space that is divisible by three in which to work it.

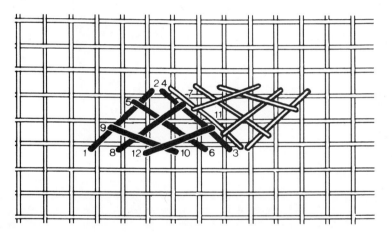

The Button Stitch

The button stitch is so called because the top cross stitch looks as if it were the stitching on a square button. It may be worked on mono-canvas but is easier to work on penelope or leno canvas. It looks very smart bordered with half cross stitches. As you work the stitch, hold the square outlining stitch out of the way so that you can include it inside your stitch, rather than stitching through it. You will be using the mesh holes it covers. This stitch cannot be halved.

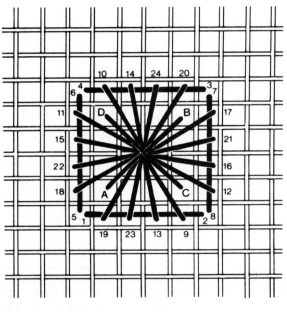

The Montenegrin Cross Stitch Adaptation

Adaptation is a polite way of saying that this is not the customary or correct way of working this stitch. The way diagramed here makes a much more interesting pattern than the proper way. A braid is produced with a bar across the throat of each V. Numbers 1 and 2 are starting stitches and are not repeated again. The sequence of the stitch is this: long cross, upright bar, short cross. If the stitch is worked in solid rows a little less wool is needed than if it is worked as a single braid. There will be quite a bit of wool on the back of the canvas.

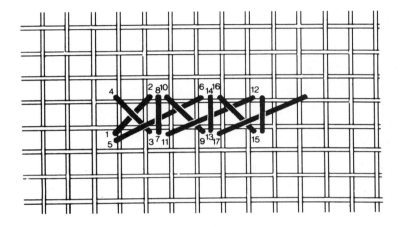

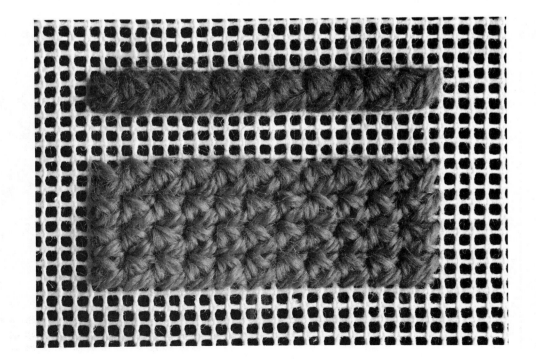

Encroaching Long Cross Stitch

Diagramed in two colors, this stitch may be worked in one if you prefer. It is a most suitable rug stitch. There will be very little wool on the back of the canvas. Work pairs of two-mesh diagonal stitches to start the stitch. The canvas will tend to buckle if you work it in large areas without a frame.

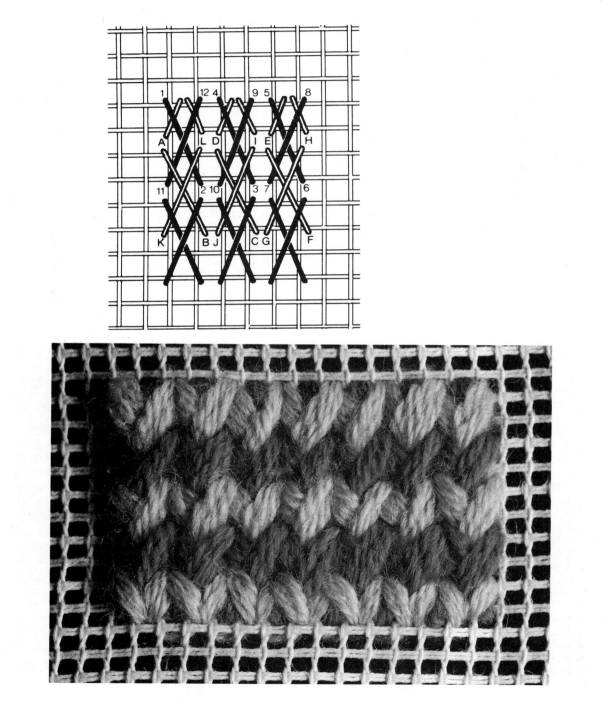

The Check Stitch

The check stitch is another super big cross stitch which looks very tweedy when worked as a grounding. If worked in diagonal rows alternating colors each stitch one can achieve a checked effect. Surprisingly you will not need more wool in your needle. Since the stitch does not halve well the space for it should be carefully planned. Be sure that you cross the stitch the same way each time.

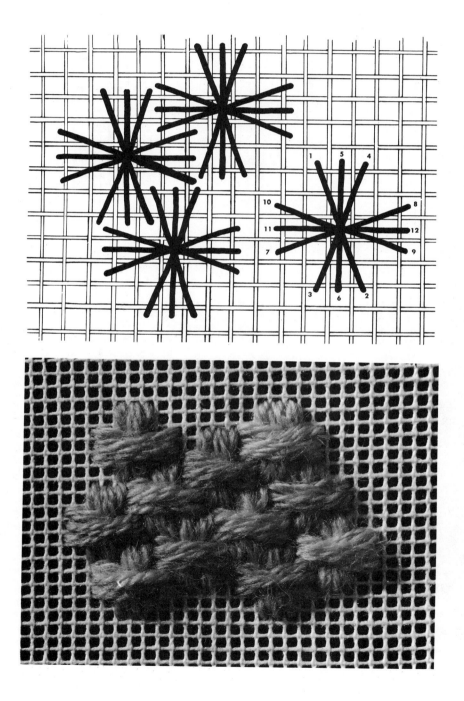

The Diagonal French Stitch

This stitch is a tall cousin of the upright cross; the result is quite different. The diagonal French stitch looks as if it were couched, as in crewel. It does not take any more wool than usual on mono-canvas and leno but you have to add more if you use it on two-thread canvas. Work the long stitches first and then go back up the row and cross them.

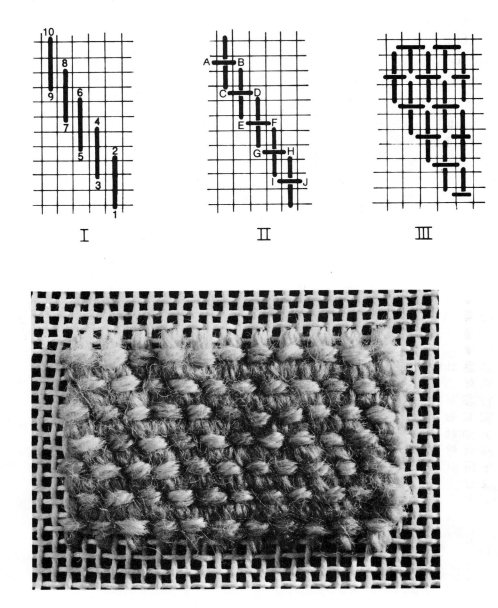

The Herringbone Stitch or the Plaited Stitch

The herringbone stitch is the head of a rather large family of related stitches, some of which don't even bear the family name, such as the plaited Gobelin, the velvet stitch, and the Bazar stitch. They all bear a family resemblance, however, in either the resulting stitch or the method used to achieve it. The basic stitch is a long stitch, slanted, with another long slanted stitch crossing it in the next stroke. All the stitches produce a rather tweedy texture except the velvet stitch which produces plush. They fit two-thread canvas the best.

The herringbone stitch is a pleasant stitch to work on the larger mesh canvases; on the smaller meshes it is hard to see just where to put the needle. It is a fine rug stitch. It must be done from left to right only, not back and forth, or you will not produce the herringbone pattern. Work a row, finish off the thread, go back to the left side and start again.

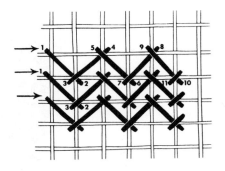

The Reverse Herringbone or
the Herringbone Gone Wrong

This member of the herringbone family is more flexible than the previous one. It is worked exactly the same except that you can work back and forth this time, from left to right and then back right to left. The result is a pretty weave on the bias. This stitch is also done on the larger mesh canvases because it is easier to get the needle down between the stitches already done. Neither stitch carries much wool on the back of the canvas.

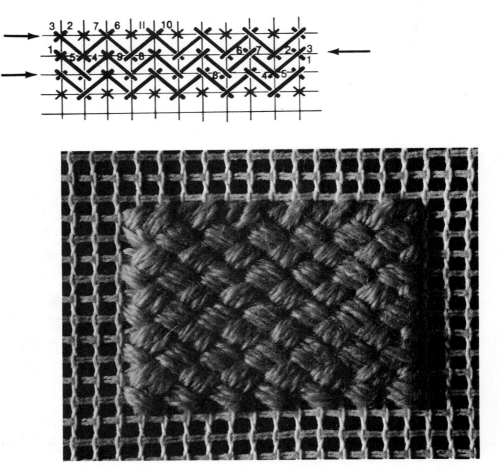

The Diagonal Reverse Herringbone Stitch

This stitch is similar in appearance to the wicker stitch but is a much tighter and more hard-wearing stitch. Working it on any canvas finer than ten mesh to the inch is a mistake but it is a good rug stitch. This is also true of its brother, the reverse herringbone. Another similarity is that you must poke back the wool on the previous row of stitches to make room for the new row. There will be little wool on the back of the canvas. Care must be taken on the outer edges of the stitch area to give it a neat woven look. Study the diagram to see how it is accomplished.

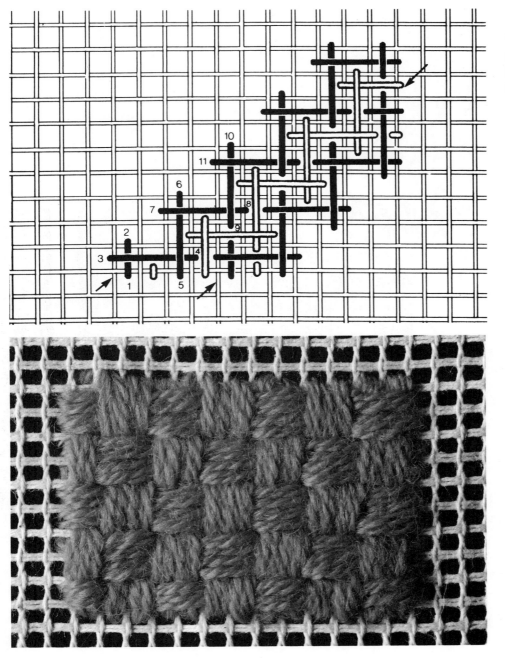

The diagram is shown in two colors for ease of reading.

The Two-Color Herringbone Stitch

This stitch is primarily used as a rug stitch but it also works well on finer mesh canvas as a separate stripe or just in rows. The foundation stitches are done in one color and then the top stitches are worked over them in another color. Of course, it may be worked in one solid color. Be careful when working this stitch to keep your stitch tension even and a little loose. Because the row of mesh in the middle of the stitch stands empty it has a tendency to buckle or squash, thereby drawing up the canvas somewhat. Loose tension will prevent this. You may want to try a little more wool in the needle than usual to cover the canvas adequately.

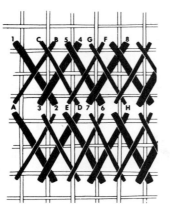

The Plaited Gobelin Stitch

The product of this stitch is a slightly more open herringbone running vertically instead of horizontally. It is worked in a different fashion from the regular herringbone but is still an easier stitch to work on large mesh canvas than fine mesh. It covers the canvas quickly and is rather fun to do. You will need to add extra wool to your needle to make this stitch cover the canvas.

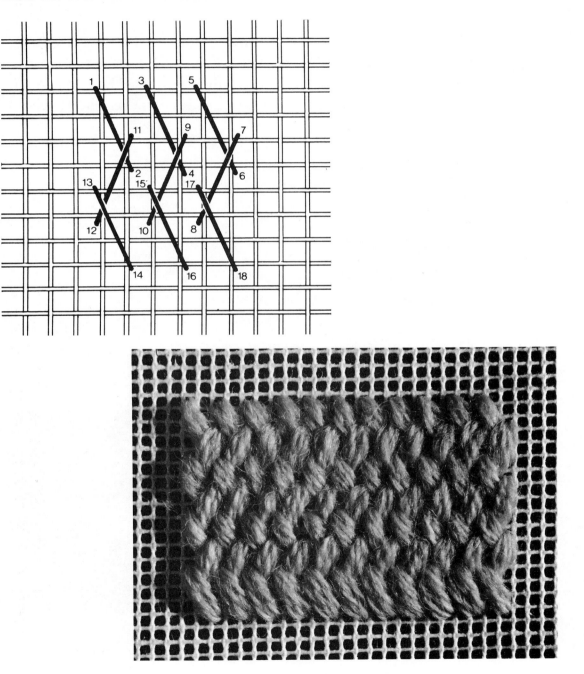

The Bazar Stitch or Six Color Herringbone Stitch

This stitch requires six journeys across the canvas to complete one row but it is worth it if you are looking for a highly decorative stitch. It should be worked on a two-thread canvas or leno canvas because it slips about on mono-canvas. The diagram shows how to start the stitch; when you have used up the four vertical mesh on which to start each row, start over again working down the vertical row. It is a very bulky stitch; you may wish to use less wool in the needle than usual. Work only from left to right. You will have to weave your wool into nearby canvas to start each row as there is little wool on the back of the canvas to help lash down. Keep your tension fairly loose to prevent the canvas underneath the stitch from buckling. Weave in any missing stitches at the beginning and the end of each row if necessary.

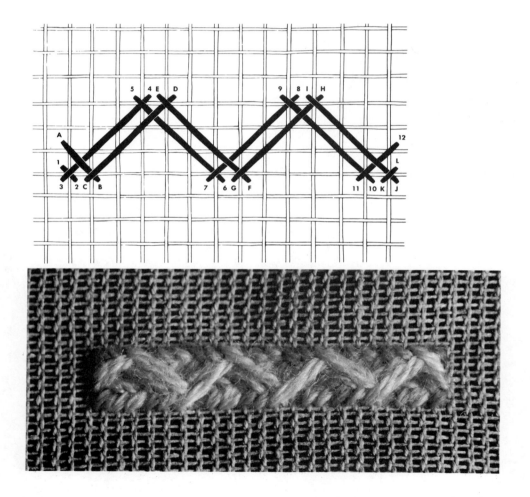

The Velvet Stitch or
the Closed Herringbone Stitch

For this stitch you'll need a little extra equipment, a strip of cardboard as long as your row of stitches will be and as wide as two mesh of the canvas you are using. This stitch is done over six mesh in height and is worked in three journeys over the same length of mesh, getting wider as one works. Work a row of herringbone stitch over two mesh of canvas using a strand less of wool than you intend to use on the outside or last row of herringbone. When completed place the long strip of cardboard over it on the face of the canvas. Work another row of herringbone over it, this time covering four mesh high with your stitches. Then work the final row of stitches six mesh high over the whole business.

On the back of the canvas, apply a coat of liquid latex such as Tri-Tix the length of the row. Allow it to dry. On the face of the canvas cut down as far as your guard strip of cardboard will allow; cut the length of the row exposing the cardboard. Remove it and hold the canvas near the steam from a tea kettle. This will make the wool fuzz nicely into a velvet-like nap. A leno or two-thread canvas is preferable over mono-canvas for this stitch.

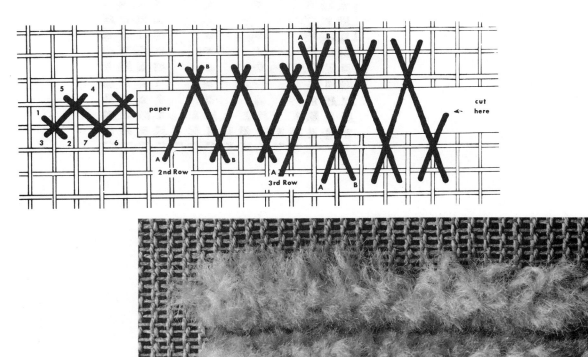

The Fern Stitch

The fern stitch makes a neat fat braid; it looks very much like a thick wale corduroy. It is quick and easy to work up and has a very thick backing. It must be worked from top to bottom only. If canvas shows between the rows either use more wool in the needle or work some little back stitches over the mesh to cover them. If you do the latter, a slightly different color gives a rather interesting effect.

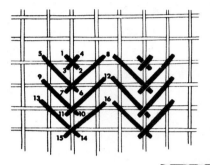

The Long and Short Oblique Stitch
or the Fishbone Stitch

This stitch is very similar to the previous one except that it looks a little lop-sided. It is just as attractive and as easy to do. Try doing the long stitch in one color and the short stitch in another color. In working the stitch one does all the long stitches first and then all of the short stitches.

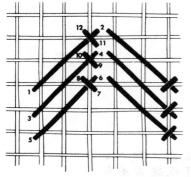

The Point de Tresse Stitch

If you want a super large braid this is the stitch to use. It can be worked on any canvas if the tension is loose enough. It is not as difficult to work as it looks. Try it as a border stitch or in stripes; it is too heavy looking for a background stitch. It is best to work the stitch as diagramed rather than carrying the wool across the back, otherwise one has as bulky a braid on the back of the canvas as on the front. In the third diagram there ARE two stitches in holes 7 and 8. The first one got there as the last stitch in diagram one.

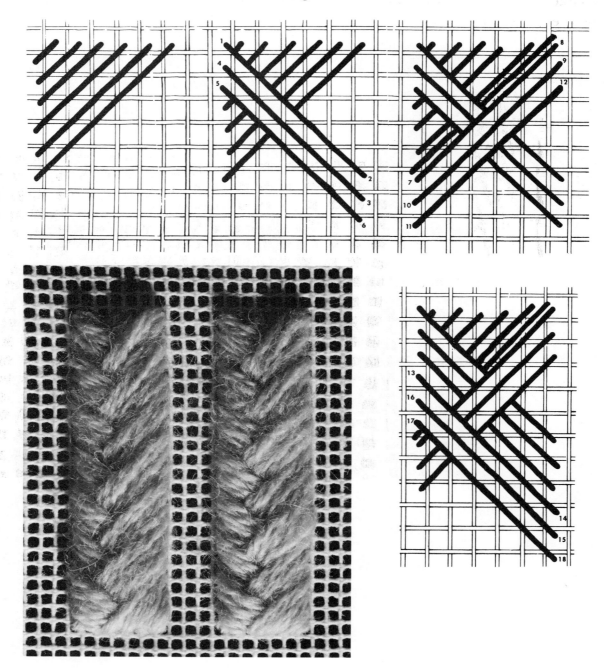

The Knotted Stitch

The knotted stitch is the first of a little group of tied-down stitches which are worked in a similar fashion. They are all basically a long stitch or long stitches with a catch stitch in the middle. The knotted stitch takes strong hands to work, but it makes a tight snag-proof surface. It can be worked in two strokes of the needle without having to put your hand under the canvas. It is worked from right to left. It has one failing which is that it draws up the canvas from side to side. Over a large area this could make quite a serious problem if your canvas is to fit a certain space, such as a church altar kneeler or a card table cover.

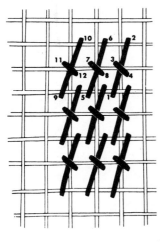

The French Stitch

The French stitch is the double tie-down stitch. It is a hard tight stitch and quite snag-proof. For a mass effect the French stitch looks neater than the Rococo stitch. It works up slowly but does not pull the canvas out of shape. It has a firm backing. Be careful of your tension so that you don't cause the canvas to buckle.

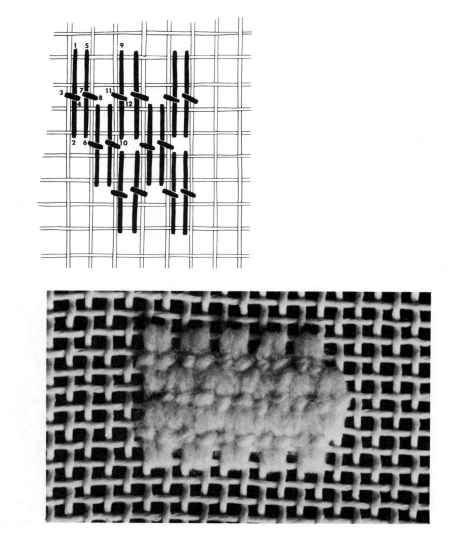

The Rococo Stitch

The Rococo stitch is one of our oldest popular stitches. It was a great favorite in the eighteenth century, both here and in England. This stitch is worked in diagonal rows. It can be used singly as a diagonal stripe on a field of half cross stitches or in rows as a backgrounding. This stitch is a terrible wool-eater.

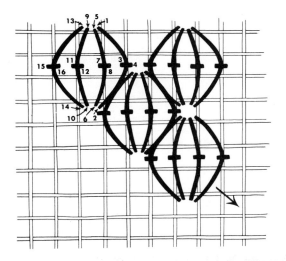

The Diagonal Shell Stitch

This stitch is the reverse of the Rococo stitch, four long stitches tied down by one. It has a thick bulky look and looks well on rugs. To cut down in the amount of wool on the back of the canvas it may be stitched in the fold way as shown in the diagram. This will also help prevent the canvas from "drawing up" thereby making that area of stitches shorter than the surrounding areas. It may be worked in vertical rows or diagonal rows but is easier to figure out worked vertically, at least until you are used to it. One must peek under the upright stitches to find where to bring the needle out to tie the stitch down. After a while you can do it by instinct. If canvas shows through at the top and bottom of the stitch, either add more wool to your needle or work a row of back stitches over the offending canvas. The stitch is quite adaptable to odd-shaped spaces since it can be halved.

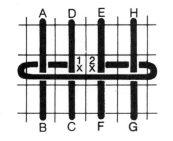

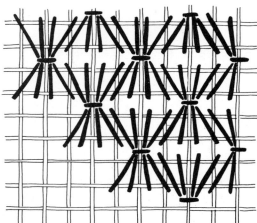

The Roumanian Stitch or the Janina Stitch

The Roumanian stitch was borrowed from crewel embroidery in the late nineteenth century and was renamed the Janina stitch. It is a very pretty member of the tied-down family but it has the bad habit of biasing the canvas. Working the stitch in a frame will control the tendency somewhat. It can be worked in two strokes on the surface of the canvas, and is worked from top to bottom. It does not look well in rows without an intervening stitch as the canvas peeks through.

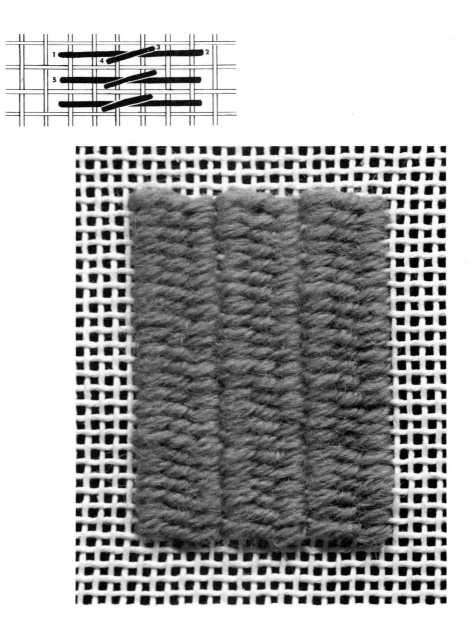

The Gobelin Stitch or the Upright Gobelin Stitch or the Straight Gobelin Stitch and the Renaissance Stitch

The Gobelin stitch is the first of a series of upright stitches, all based more or less on the same idea, a vertical stitch between the mesh. They all have the same traits. They cover the canvas quickly but are notorious wool-eaters! The reasons for this latter trait are two-fold. In order to cover the canvas adequately it is necessary to add extra strands of wool to the needle. Then to make the stitches lie flat and straight, it is advisable to stitch so that there is as much wool on the back of the canvas as on the face. Wool does not like to bend, it prefers to coil. (See diagram.) Stitches that are not coil stitches will gap and lie "open" like the pages of an open book.

Try to keep the strand of wool untwisted as you work; the stitch looks neater untwisted and the wool is fatter when lying straight. It is very hard not to have canvas show between rows of the Gobelin stitch; however it combines nicely with alternating rows of any of the braid-like stitches such as the Greek stitch or the running cross stitch.

You can tramé this stitch and then it is called the Renaissance stitch. The tramé will beef it up and give it a pronounced ridge. Tramé unevenly along every other horizontal weft thread on mono-canvas, and between every pair of weft threads on penelope canvas.

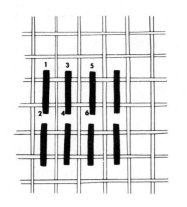 The Gobelin Stitch

 Wool coiling

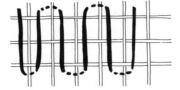 Wool bending

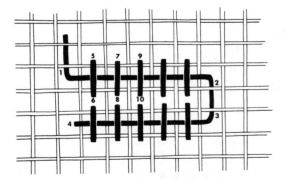

 The Renaissance Stitch

The Gobelin Tramé Stitch

This stitch is a variation of the Gobelin stitch also. When it appeared in *Peterson's Magazine* in 1856 it was suggested that the tramé be done in braid, gold or silver, or straw. The key to success with this stitch is to have the tramé wool (or other thread) completely cover the two threads of mesh over which the upright Gobelin will be worked. You will have to experiment to achieve this. The tramé is worked row by row, just ahead of your Gobelin stitches. In this stitch, it is laid over an entire row of mesh, tucked into the canvas at the end of the row and then emerges for the next row of tramé. It is worked this way to keep the gaps of regular tramé from showing, which would spoil the woven look, and to keep the tension on the tramé thread loose enough.

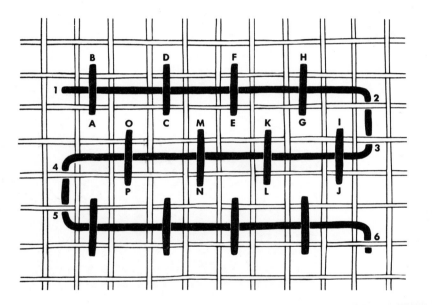

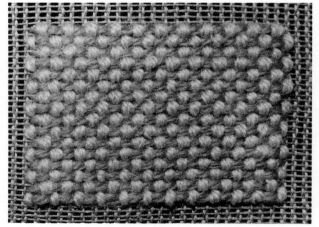

The Brick Stitch or the Alternating Stitch

The brick stitch is an excellent background stitch and is very easy to work. As with the other upright stitches you will have to experiment with your wool until you have added enough threads to cover the canvas. Use only leno canvas or mono-canvas for this stitch. Because two-thread canvases have too much space between their two threads, the upright brick stitch cannot spread out enough to cover the space. This is true of all of the upright stitches on two-thread canvases.

There are two ways to work the brick stitch. The first way is used just to cover the ground quickly. It is stitched diagonally so be careful your tension is even or a ridge of stitches will result. The first way is more economical with wool than the second way.

The second way is stitched horizontally, back and forth from left to right, and right to left. The canvas will bias if all the rows are worked from the same direction. The advantage of the second way is that it provides such a firm backing to the canvas. This is important if you are making a wall hanging or a rug and are using the basket weave stitch or some other heavily backed stitch. If a heavily backed stitch is worked next to a lightly backed stitch, the canvas will ripple in the lightly backed area. This will not block out. This would be most unfortunate on a rug border, for instance.

To give a clean edge to the stitch where it meets another kind of stitch, just work upright stitches over one mesh.

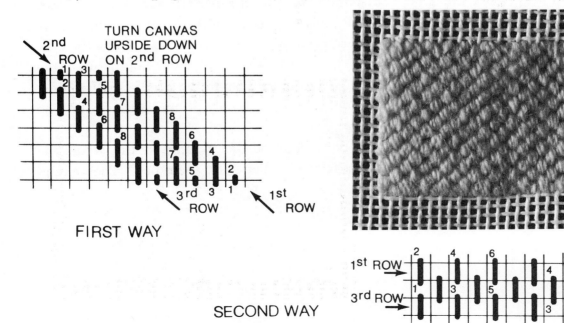

FIRST WAY

SECOND WAY

Bargello or the Florentine Stitch
or Florentine Embroidery or the Flame Stitch

Bargello, as it is popularly called, is THE most popular stitch of all the fancy needlepoint stitches. It is also one of the oldest, having been used since the seventeenth century. It is a long upright stitch worked in "stair-step" patterns in progressive colors which repeat themselves to form a pattern. The most common count for a bargello stitch is four mesh high, with the next stitch occurring two mesh higher or lower on the canvas. This is called a four two step. Another combination could be six mesh high with the next stitch occurring two mesh lower or higher; this would be a six two step. The next row beneath follows the pattern set up by the first row. To show off the pattern each row is done in a different color or shade, with the sequence of colors repeating themselves down the canvas. This is what causes the flame-like appearance to the stitch. There are other variations, however, that are not flame-like but look like hearts, fish-scales, trees and diamonds. If the pattern is a peaked flame-like one, there is usually a center peak with the left side of the pattern being a mirror image of the right.

Set up your bargello canvas by folding it in half and running a basting thread up the fold. This will insure that the pattern will come out evenly on each side. With this stitch you count the HOLES between the mesh horizontally to plot the pattern across the canvas. Count the canvas threads vertically to figure the length of each stitch. Expect to use about a third more wool in your needle to cover the canvas. There should be no "lice" (a tapestry term) showing between the horizontal rows. If there is, add more wool to the needle until you get rid of them! Bargello should be worked only on mono-canvas or leno canvas.

It is important to twirl your needle to untwist the wool; the stitches should lie flat to cover and to look their best. The tension

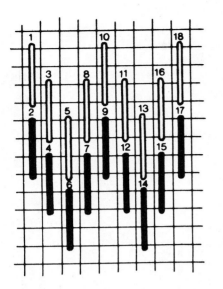

A Simple Bargello Pattern

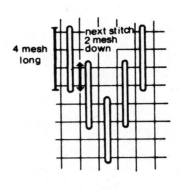

A 4/2 Step

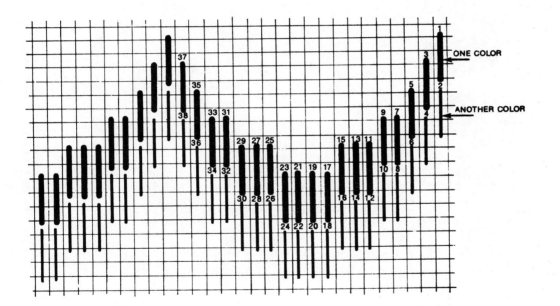

A Bargello wave pattern

should be fairly loose for this stitch; if your basket weave stitching is too tight, bargello will help you to loosen it up. As with the brick stitch, coil your stitches rather than bend them.

There are many excellent books available just on bargello patterns or try making up your own, which is really fun.

If you only have two-thread canvas or penelope, and you are eager to try bargello, try working a long cross stitch over the warp threads. Be sure you slant the top stitches in the same direction. You will be surprised how many people will think it is true bargello.

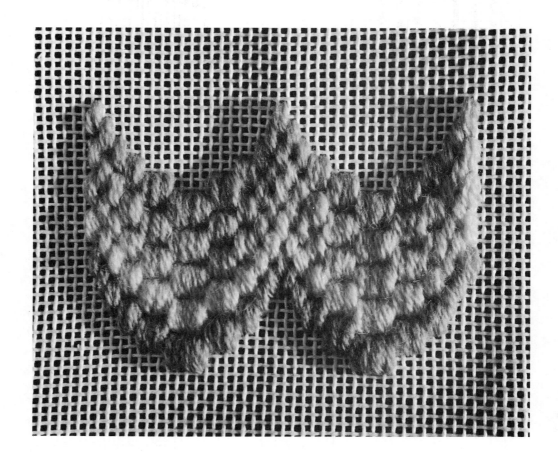

The Old Florentine Stitch

This stitch is a set pattern stitch of the bargello type. It may be worked in just one color or in alternating rows of two or more colors. It is not very snag-proof in that the long stitches cover nine mesh, but it does work up quickly for the same reason. Be sure that there is enough wool in your needle; about a third more than usual may be necessary.

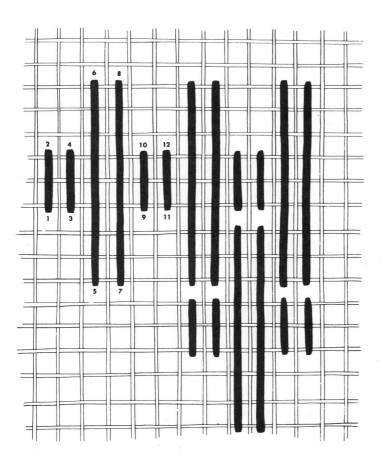

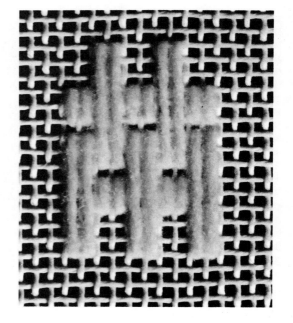

The Irish Stitch

The Irish stitch is an overgrown brick stitch and would be used the same way. It can be stitched the same ways the brick stitch is, and it too will require more wool in the needle to cover the canvas adequately. They look rather well together on the same piece of work. Make sure your wool is not twisted tightly as you stitch; each stitch should lie flat, fat, and even. Just twirl the needle in your fingers every few stitches; this will prevent it from twisting too much. The other thing to watch with this stitch is that your tension is loose enough to prevent the canvas from buckling or "taking up." Stitch a test swatch of a few square inches if it is important that the canvas not be foreshortened. If you find that your stitches draw up the canvas, work the Irish stitch in a frame.

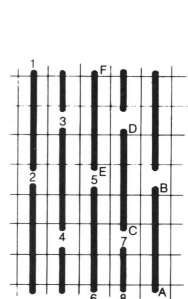

The Parisian Embroidery Stitch

This stitch has a close cousin, the Hungarian embroidery stitch, and they are hard to tell apart at first. They are both worked over two and four mesh but in different combinations; compare the diagrams and you will see. This cousin forms a stripe, while the other forms a diamond. This stitch looks equally well in one color or in alternating colors. More wool will be required to cover the canvas for both of these stitches. If you work it back and forth from right to left, then vice versa, the canvas is less apt to bias.

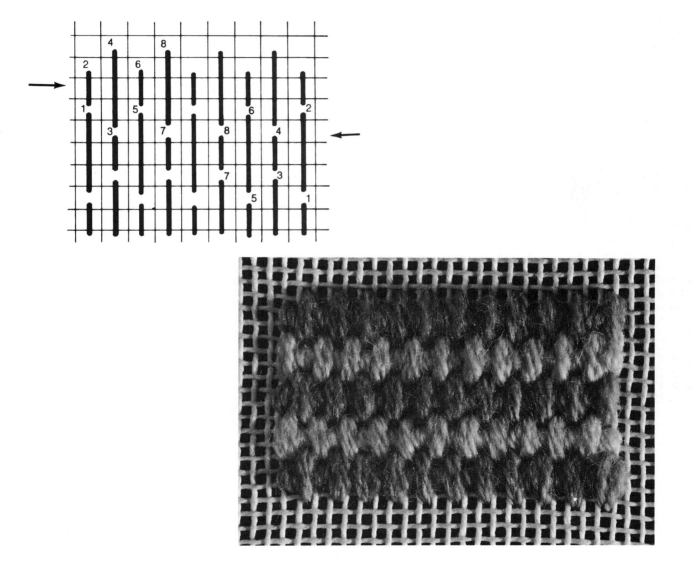

The Hungarian Embroidery Stitch

The Hungarian embroidery stitch is the trickier of the two related stitches, the other being the Parisian embroidery stitch. The reason for this is that one works three upright stitches to form the diamond and then a space is skipped before the next diamond is commenced. Once the pattern is set in the first row, the stitch becomes easier. This stitch is pretty done in two colors; it gives a diagonal checkerboard effect.

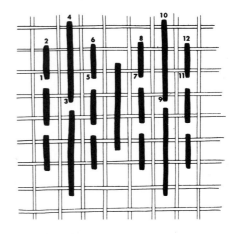

The Shaded Stripe Stitch

With this stitch you get a six mesh wide stripe for the price of four mesh. That is because there is no stitch longer than four mesh; this means a little less snagability (if there is such a word). Work the long stitches first and then fill in the short ones from side to side. Again, with this stitch one must be careful to work with an even tension or the canvas will buckle.

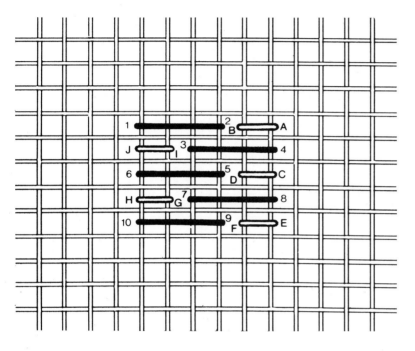

The Enlarged Parisian Embroidery Stitch

The enlarged Parisian embroidery stitch has a tie-down stitch which makes it less snag-prone than it would be otherwise with that long six mesh center stitch. The tie-down stitch, please note, is made from the same hole in the canvas; come up, go over the center stitch and then pop the needle back down the same hole from which you emerged. Worked over a large area this stitch does tend to bias the canvas, so a frame would be recommended. The stitch halves nicely which makes it more versatile for odd size spaces. You will need a third more wool in your needle for this stitch than you would for the half cross stitch on the same canvas. It has a very firm backing.

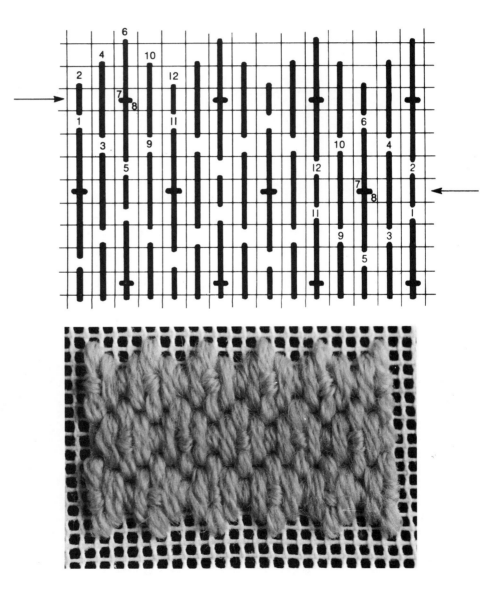

The Wicker Stitch

The wicker stitch looks like basket work. It can be used by itself for the pretty pattern or as an interesting texture stitch. It covers the canvas quickly and does not bias the canvas. Be consistent in the way you work this stitch; either coil the wool or bend it but not both on the same canvas. Bulges and ripples will be the result if you mix the stitch technique.

As you work each set of three stitches it is a good idea to hold back with your thumb the last stitch of the last set worked. This will expose more clearly the mesh that you will be working on next. To fill the gap that shows on the outside edge of a finished block of stitches, work a little row of half cross stitch or upright stitches over one mesh. Work this stitch only on mono-canvas or leno canvas.

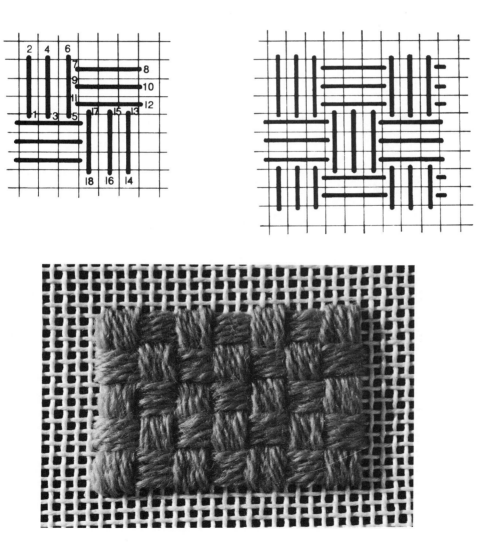

The Diagonal Wicker Stitch

This stitch and the reverse herringbone stitch resemble each other quite a bit. They are worked in a different manner, however, and this one produces a larger diagonal weave. It is shown in two colors to make it easier for you to follow. It really looks best in just one color, giving a hand-woven basket effect.

Begin the stitch as diagramed, then come back and fill in the space to your bottom edge. It will take two rows of stitching to edge off. Be careful that you don't pull too tightly on the wool or the canvas will buckle. You will need a space for it that is divisible by four in each direction. It can be worked in irregularly shaped spaces if you are patient enough to work it out. You must peek under completed stitches to find the holes for the next row of stitches. This stitch is not a good one for a beginner to tackle, nor is it recommended for fine mesh canvas.

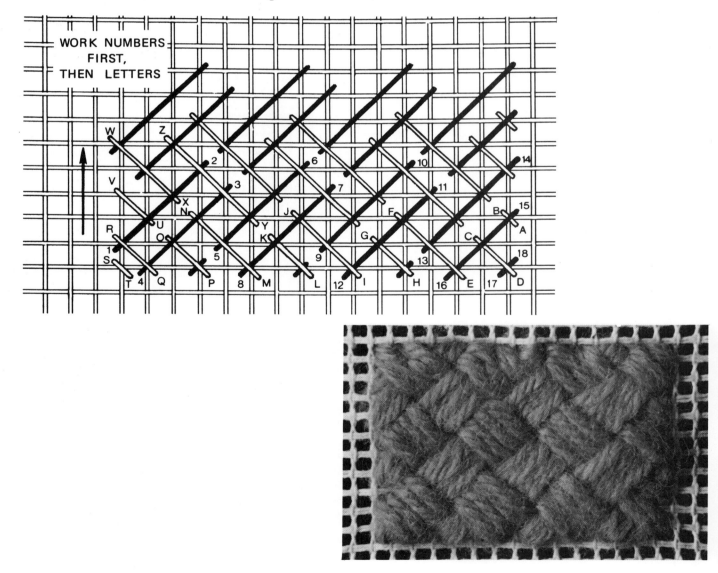

The Slanting Gobelin Stitch

The slanting Gobelin stitch is the simplest of all the slanting stitches. As a general rule the slanting stitches do not require extra wool in the needle to cover the canvas the way the upright stitches do. This stitch can be used over up to five horizontal threads or over two vertical threads as well as one. It has a very firm backing but will bias the canvas somewhat if worked over large areas. A frame is recommended.

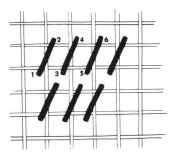

The Interlocking Gobelin Stitch or the Encroaching Gobelin Stitch

This stitch and the two following it are very much alike; they differ only in the way they are stroked or in the number of mesh they cover. The stem stitch in crewel embroidery is probably the original source.

The interlocking Gobelin stitch is a most attractive stitch; it works up quickly, makes a smooth hard surface on the face of the canvas and a nice thick back. However, it does bias the canvas and if you work your stitches tightly it will draw up the canvas. This means that the canvas will be shorter than you intended. Therefore if you are a tight stitcher, a frame is recommended.

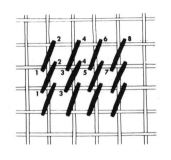

The Encroaching Oblique Stitch or the Soumak Stitch

This stitch may be worked vertically or horizontally, whichever is more comfortable for you. It differs from the previous stitch in that it is stitched more like the stem stitch and not in horizontal rows. If worked in large amounts it will bias the canvas somewhat so a frame is recommended. It makes a rather nice background stitch if there are not too many small nooks and crannies it must be fitted into. At the beginning and end of each row work a two-mesh stitch to fill in the gap.

The Oblique Slav Stitch

The oblique Slav stitch is worked diagonally. If you will compare it to the encroaching oblique stitch you will see the similarity; this stitch is just two mesh higher. It is rather difficult to understand at first but quite simple to do once you catch on! The stitch works best with a fat amount of wool on a finer mesh canvas. Since there is not much wool on the back of the canvas it is fairly economical with wool. Its fault is that it is not very snag-proof.

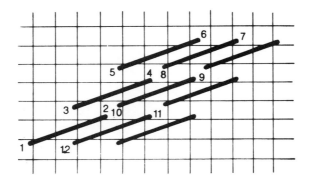

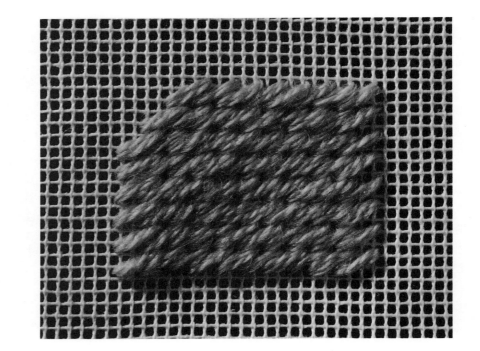

The Kalem Stitch or the Knit Stitch
or the Knitting Stitch or the Reverse Tent Stitch

This is one of the best background stitches there is. It also does well for details in small areas; you can even outline in the stitch. For years rugs have been made in Greece using the knit stitch exclusively. It can be worked so that the texture runs vertically, horizontally or if you choose, diagonally; see the following stitch description. If you look at the stitch closely you will see that it is really just the continental stitch worked wrong-side-to and in two different directions. The stitch does not bias the canvas very much because the different directions of the slant correct the tendency.

Work a half cross stitch at the beginning and end of each row slanting in the OPPOSITE direction than the row is to go. This will give a clean line to the edge of the stitch. This stitch takes just a little less wool than the half cross stitch would on the same canvas. It should be stroked in and out with one thrust on the surface of the canvas, however the canvas will have to be turned around and around as one must do with the continental stitch.

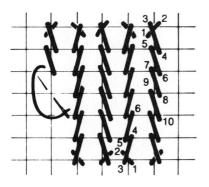

The Diagonal Knit Stitch

This companion to the knit stitch may be worked in either direction; just turn the book half way around to make it slant towards the left. One really has to think about this stitch to get the hang of it. In large amounts it will bias the canvas so a frame is recommended.

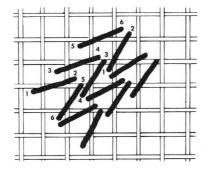

The Mosaic Stitch or the German Stitch

Here is another excellent background stitch, particularly if you are looking for a very small patterned stitch. It looks quite well as a border stitch also. It has a firm backing and will accommodate itself to any canvas. If you are going to be working very large areas of the mosaic stitch the canvas will bias if you stitch it tightly. In this case a frame would be recommended.

Working the stitch as diagramed below will reduce the tendency to bias that will occur if you work each little "mosaic" separately. Work the small stitches first, basket weave style, and then work the long strokes in random horizontal or vertical rows. Do not work them in diagonally; this will increase the bias pull if you do.

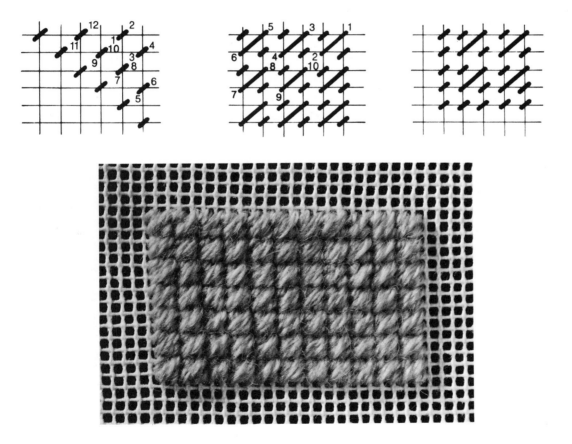

The Mosaic Stitch Done Diagonally or the Diagonal Florentine Stitch

This variation of the mosaic stitch makes a good background stitch also, but it does bias the canvas. A frame is strongly recommended. Try working it in alternating stripes using two colors. It is not too much of a wool-eater.

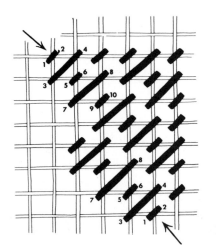

The Cashmere Stitch

The cashmere stitch has a neat embossed look about it; it makes a nice background stitch if you want a little pattern to it. It does not bias the canvas as much as the Scotch stitch but a frame would be recommended for large areas of it. It is rather fun to work, especially if you stitch it diagonally as shown in the diagram.

The Cashmere Stitch Worked Diagonally

If you happen to be looking for a stitch that looks like water ripples, this is the one. It is a nice stitch for other uses too, of course, but it is especially suited for water effects. It does bias the canvas somewhat, so for large areas use a frame. Work it diagonally as shown.

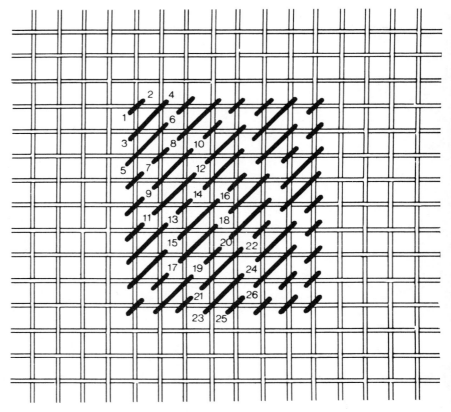

The Brick Cashmere Stitch

Here is another variation of an old favorite. It can be stitched in one solid color but it will display its pattern more effectively in two colors. If it is to be worked over a large area of canvas, an embroidery frame is recommended. Try to stitch cleanly into each mesh so that you do not nibble into the wool already there. This will make a crisper outline. There will be a fair amount of wool on the back of the canvas with this stitch.

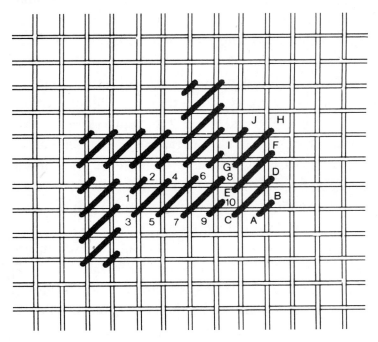

The Scotch Stitch and the Checker Stitch and the Point Russe Stitch

The Scotch stitch is a great favorite with needlepointers because it is attractive and versatile. It can be used by itself and in combination with other stitches to form interesting patterns. For instance, the Scotch square may be turned around so that it slants in four different directions, the whole thing can then be bordered with half cross stitch, or each square can be bordered with half cross stitch. The Point Russe stitch is a variation of the Scotch stitch using four halves of the stitch backed into each other and sometimes delineated by four long stitches. It is best used as a specimen stitch or alternately with squares of half cross stitch because when it is used as a grounding it looks just like a field of Scotch stitch unless every other stitch is a different color.

Alternating squares of half cross stitch with squares of Scotch stitch will form a checker-like pattern. This pattern is sometimes called the checker stitch. Another variation to make the stitch a little more snag-proof is to weave the needle over and under the stitch to create a woven effect. Always weave in the same direction; try using a weaving thread of a different color than the square itself.

If you work more than just a couple of rows of this stitch, an embroidery frame should be used. It is one of the greatest canvas biasers of all time. In addition to the frame, be sure you stitch with a slightly loose tension. You are literally tying the canvas into a slanted position as you stitch, and if it is stitched tightly there will be no hope of ever blocking it straight.

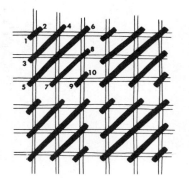

The Scotch Stitch

Variations on the Scotch Stitch

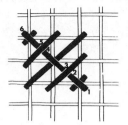

Woven Scotch Stitch

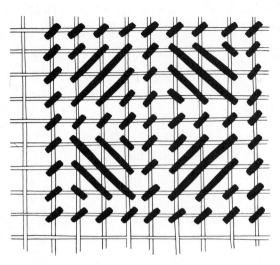

Scotch Stitch bordered with half cross stitches

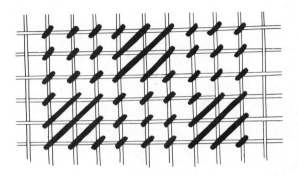

The Checker Stitch

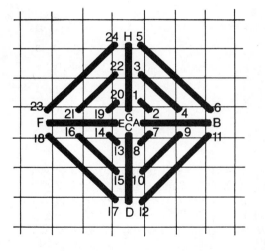

The Point Russe Stitch

86

The Scotch Stitch Worked Diagonally or the Diagonal Stitch and the Moorish Stitch

This stitch has a fat padded look to it, perhaps because it is almost padded. There is as much wool on the back of the canvas as on the front; furthermore a little more wool is needed in the needle in order to cover the canvas properly. The pattern does not lead the eye too strongly because the steps of the stitch are short. Like its parent stitch, it does bias the canvas and a frame should be used.

If a row of half cross stitch is worked between each diagonal row of the stepped stitches the stitch is called the Moorish stitch.

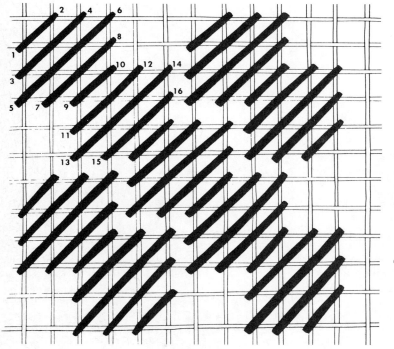

The Scotch Stitch worked diagonally

The Moorish Stitch

The Byzantine Stitch and the Jacquard Stitch

The Byzantine stitch is fairly easy to do once the first zigzag stripe is worked from top to bottom. After that you just follow the steps it made. The simplest way to do the stitch is from left to right. It does not pull the canvas out of shape as much as the other diagonal stitches. Try it in very strong colors.

The same stitch with a separating row of half cross stitch worked between each diagonal stripe is called the Jacquard stitch. Both stitches may be enlarged by adding more stitches on the horizontal and vertical steps.

The Leaf Stitch

The leaf stitch is one of the most attractive and unusual of the fancy stitches. It is not particularly hard to do, has a nice backing and does not use an inordinate amount of wool. Its only drawback is that it is not very snag-proof as diagramed. However, the stitch can be reduced as shown in the accompanying diagram. An upright stitch can be inserted on the leaf to resemble the main stem if desired. This stitch makes a very attractive border (see diagram) and is also handsome worked just by itself as a pillow or purse. You may have to use a little extra wool in your needle to cover the canvas.

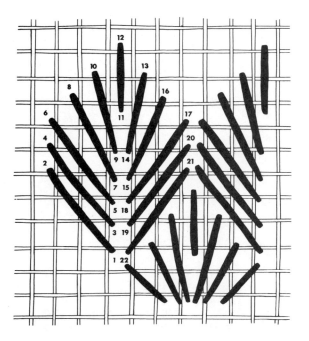

The Leaf Stitch

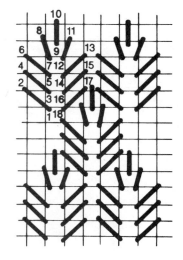

The Leaf Stitch modified

The Leaf Stitch used as a border

The Stem Stitch or the Long Oblique Stitch with Running Stitch and the Perspective Stitch

The stem stitch is another corduroy-like stitch, simple to do and with a fairly firm backing. It can be worked in two colors very effectively, the oblique stitches in one color, the running stitches in another. Use less wool in your needle for the running stitches than you do for the oblique. Put a half cross stitch at the beginning of each row, worked in the same direction as the following stitches, to close the little gap. Do the same at the end of each row.

The perspective stitch does not use the running stitch, just three pairs of oblique stitches overlapping three more pairs of oblique stitches heading in the opposite direction. This stitch may be worked in one color, but it needs two colors to show the "box" illusion of the stitch. The wool must fit the canvas exactly on this stitch or the canvas will show through in the center. Experiment until no canvas shows.

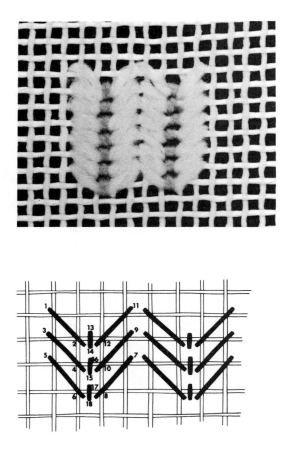

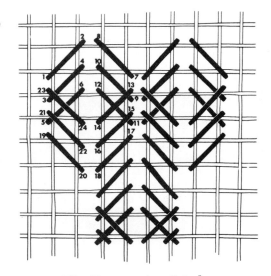

The Perspective Stitch

The Milanese Stitch and the Oriental Stitch

Another great canvas-biaser, the Milanese stitch enjoys great popularity because of the attractive pattern it forms. It is not very snag-proof either. Use a frame if you plan to work large areas of it. Working the stitch from the diagram below is rather like patting your head and rubbing your tummy, but it will cut down on the bias tendency. The stitch can be reduced in size and the effect retained by omitting that last long stitch and making it just three strokes long.

The oriental stitch is a variation of the Milanese stitch with a three stroke addition between each diagonal stripe of triangles. It is effective only if worked in two different colors.

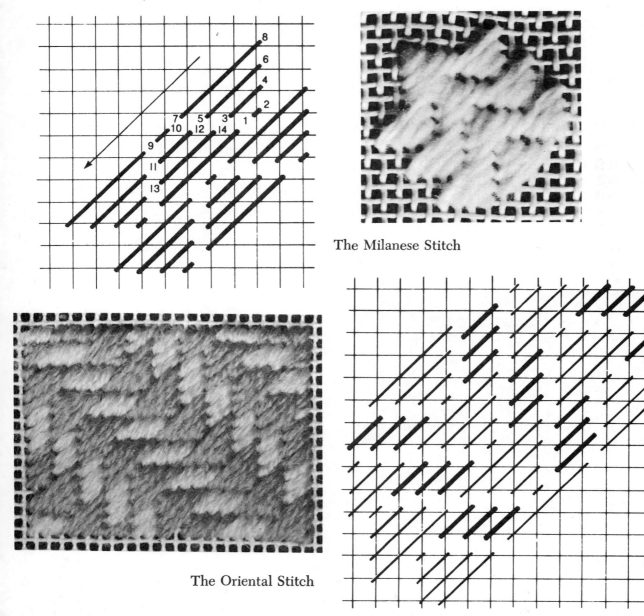

The Milanese Stitch

The Oriental Stitch

The Star Stitch or the Algerian Eye Stitch and the Eye Stitch and the Ray Stitch

The star stitch is the basic model of the following eight stitches. They are all ray or spoke stitches radiating out of one central mesh. They must be stitched very carefully or they will have a lumpy appearance. The star stitch is best worked on a two-thread canvas or a leno canvas. The stitch makes a flat square pattern. It is rather slow working up because you have to keep going back to the center mesh over and over. If the wool does not fit the canvas just right it will show through; however, you will find that you will need less wool rather than more. If the wool is too fat it is difficult to pull the needle through the same center mesh again and again.

If you enlarge the basic star stitch to four, six or even eight mesh the result is the eye stitch. It is difficult to work this stitch so that it has a neat appearance. The last stitch always seems to stand higher than the others.

The ray stitch is the eye stitch quartered. It should be worked over three mesh each way to have any definition at all. The rays may radiate all in the same direction or alternate, first to the right then to the left. The stitch covers the canvas best if the rays all radiate in the same direction. The ray stitch does bias the canvas somewhat.

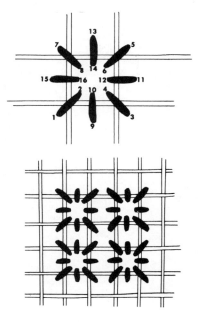

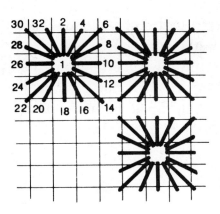

The Eye Stitch

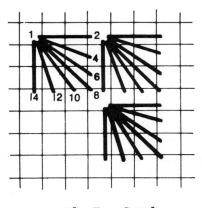

The Ray Stitch

The Diamond Eyelet Stitch

This stitch is another one where you must be careful to fit the wool just right to the canvas. If the wool is too thin the canvas will show through on the outer rays. Work the stitch in the same sequence for every diamond; a swirl effect is created and it should be consistent. On the diagram there are no odd numbers; they are all in the center at number 1. A running stitch may be used to outline the diamonds.

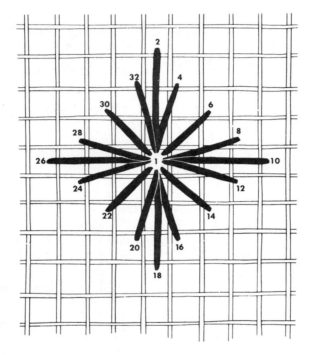

The Reverse Eyelet Stitch

This stitch must be combined with the half cross stitch to retain its identity. If it is worked in an all-over field it just looks like an eyelet stitch. The diagram shows the stitch plain, and then the lower right shows it quartered with a long stitch. The long stitch will cover up any "lice" showing through if the wool doesn't quite fit the canvas. You will need to work a square six half cross stitches by six half cross stitches to have the checker effect work out correctly.

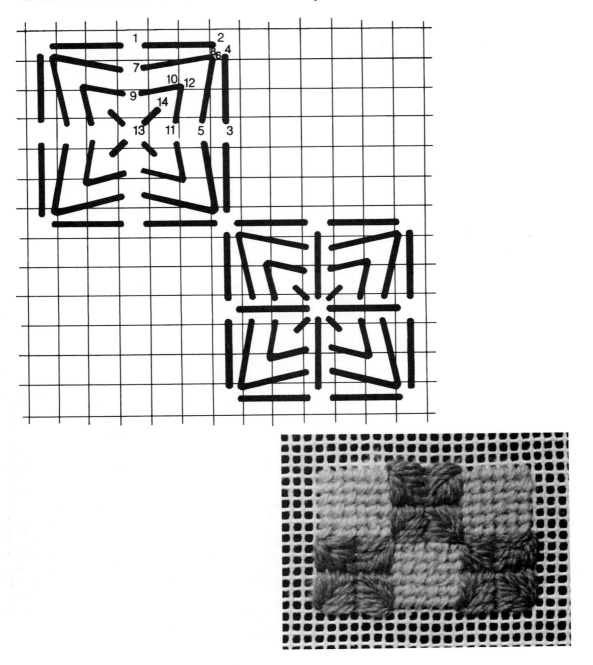

The Triangle Stitch

The triangle stitch is a splashy geometric stitch. It is not very snag-proof but it does have a good firm backing. It cannot be used alone without the help of a cross stitch in each corner; otherwise there would be empty canvas there. Another way of filling this empty space is applicable if you are working a field of triangle stitches. Work all the triangle stitches, then fill those four four-mesh-by-four-mesh gaps with a double leviathan stitch. The triangle stitch sort of belongs to the upright stitch family; therefore it will not look well on a two-thread or penelope canvas. You may need more wool in your needle to cover the canvas.

The Triple Leviathan Stitch

The triple leviathan stitch is a very decorative stitch that may be used by itself as a specimen stitch surrounded by half cross stitches or as an all-over pattern stitch in horizontal rows. It shows itself off to best advantage on a fairly large mesh canvas. Try it in two colors, the rays in one color and the crosses in another color. Make sure all the crosses cross in the same direction. You may find that less wool in the needle will give a tidier look to the ray stitches.

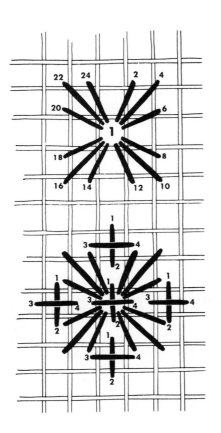

The Flower Stitch

The flower stitch can only be used as a specimen stitch; it cannot be used as a grounding stitch. It looks best if the half cross stitch surrounding it is worked in four different directions (see diagram). Work the outer stitches first, using a little less wool than you would ordinarily. Work the center cross stitches last, using the usual amount of wool. Then work the surrounding half cross stitches.

The Web Stitch

This stitch may best be described as tramé worked diagonally. The result does not look like needlepoint, it has a more woven appearance, very close and hard. It is advisable to do this stitch on a fairly large mesh for the sake of your eyesight. It works up very slowly, and therefore would never do as a background stitch because it is so tedious. It is mainly a special effects or accent stitch. Work a row of the diagonal tramé first, then cover it with the half cross stitches. Hold the canvas so that the tramé stitches are parallel to your body. You can follow the half cross stitch placement better that way.

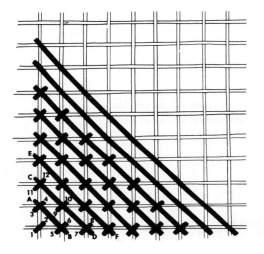

The Darning Stitch

The darning stitch is basically a rug stitch but with today's products it would be rather hard to work; rug wool is just too bulky. It fits a large mesh mono-canvas using tapestry wool much better. Persian wool is satisfactory too. You will have to experiment to see just what works best for you. The stitch is a great wool-eater and is not very snag-proof. It is worked in four trips across the canvas using the same set of holes. Go over four canvas threads and under two to the end of your allotted space. On the return trip you will go over the canvas threads that you went under the last trip, and under the threads you went over. Make these journeys back and forth once more and the stitch is completed. The diagram shows on the right side how to handle an uneven number of mesh.

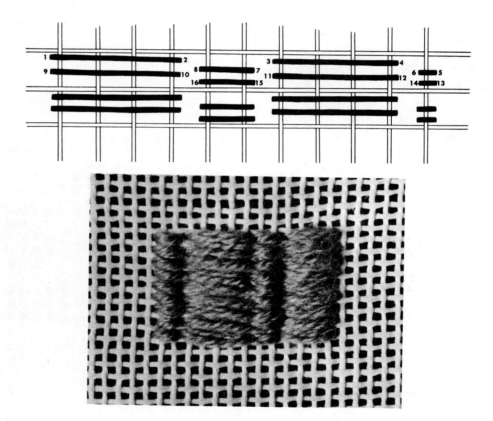

Turkey Work

Turkey work is the first of three shaggy and knotted stitches which are excellent rug stitches and are also wonderful accent stitches. They can be used to give a lion a mane, a doll hair, or a squirrel a tail. This version, turkey work, can be worked on any canvas. On a two-thread canvas, a single stitch can be worked over one set of mesh to make a very dense pile. The stitch is usually worked over two threads of mono-canvas or leno canvas and over two sets of threads of two-thread canvas. To keep the turkey work pile from working its way into nearby stitches, complete all your other stitching before you start the turkey work. The space allotted for turkey work must be divisible by two, because each complete stitch uses two mesh. If you have one mesh over, work one surrey stitch there; it is the following stitch. No extra wool is needed in your needle for any of these pile stitches. Work the turkey work stitch from the bottom of the canvas up. It can be worked in either direction, right to left or left to right, whichever is the most comfortable for you. Use your thumb as the gauge to measure the pile and also to hold the wool down as you work the next stitch. Do not cut the pile until all the stitches are completed. Then trim with scissors. If you fear that small fingers will unpluck some pile, paint the back of the turkey work with a light coat of liquid latex. If you hold the cut pile over a steam kettle it will frizz nicely.

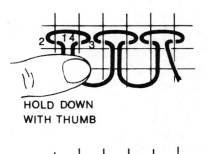

HOLD DOWN
WITH THUMB

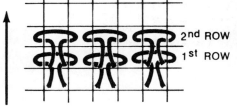

2nd ROW
1st ROW

The Surrey Stitch

The surrey stitch is the same stroke pattern as turkey work; it is just done over an intersection of mesh instead of a pair of threads. The stitch slides about a bit on mono-canvas as it is being worked but is all right once the knot is pulled tight. The surrey stitch is also worked from the bottom of the canvas up. Don't cut the pile until you have completed all your stitches. The length of the pile should be about three quarters of an inch long before cutting. You can trim it or really mow it down shorter.

To start the stitch bring the needle in and out of the canvas as in diagram **a.** Holding down with your thumb the tag of wool left out, bring the needle and wool around to the left. Insert it from the right into the hole next door as in diagrams **b** and **c.** The needle must pass over its own tail, so to speak, to form the knot. To start the next stitch insert the needle at X as in diagram **d.** To start the next row begin in the row of mesh just above the row completed.

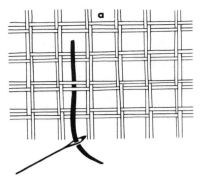

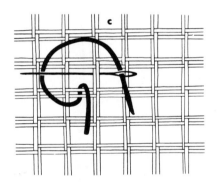

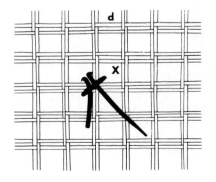

The Raised Work Stitch

This version of the plush stitch was popular in the nineteenth century. If you need just a row or two of a shaggy stitch this is the one to use. The other two versions, turkey work and the surrey stitch, are so much easier to stitch. This one is a little tedious, but does have a nice finished look to it because of the half cross stitch that locks it down. The half cross stitch also helps it to slant in one direction, perfect for a fringe.

You will probably need a little less wool in your needle than usual. It works most comfortably on leno or two-thread canvas. Start this stitch from the bottom of the canvas as you do for the other two, working from left to right up the canvas. Secure the loop or fringe with your non-needle-wielding thumb as you work the locking half cross stitch. As with the other two plush stitches, this stitch should be the last stitch worked on the canvas. Work all the raised work stitches, then cut the loops open with your scissors. Trim to the length you desire. The steam from a tea kettle will give a nice fuzzy look to the wool.

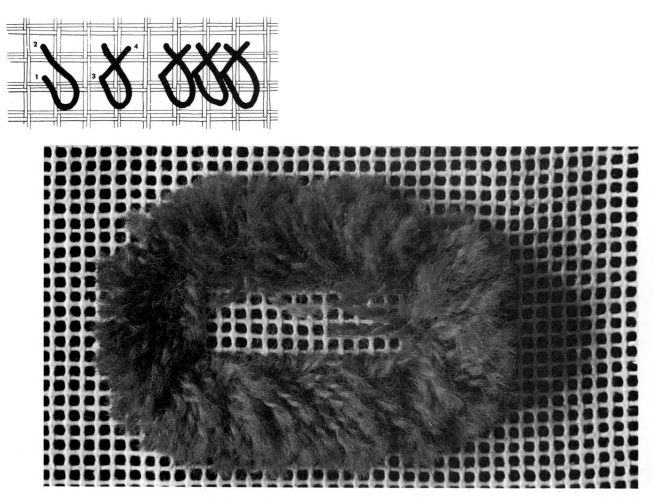

The Chain Stitch

The chain stitch does not look like needlepoint; it looks like knitting. Each stitch ties down the stitch before it. It takes some experimenting to get the wool to fit the canvas exactly, the problem being to have the wool thin enough not to crowd the mesh together as the stitch is worked. At the same time the wool must be fat enough to cover the canvas. Penelope canvas or two-thread canvas will accommodate this stitch better than mono-canvas. The chain stitch is worked from top to bottom only. Include the loop of the last stitch worked on each new stitch. Loop the wool under the needle to form the next stitch. To finish a row bring the needle up in the center of the last loop, and then down again over the next horizontal mesh. Run the needle through the backs of nearby stitches to anchor the wool. This means that at the end of each chain of stitches you must finish off the thread and then start fresh at the beginning of the next row.

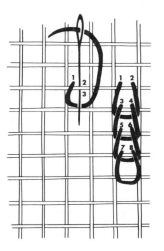

The Laced Chain Stitch

To start this stitch one must work a row of upright Gobelin stitch; work two stitches in every other mesh. For the next row, bring the needle to the surface of the canvas one row of mesh down and beneath an empty mesh. Pick up one Gobelin stitch from the pairs on either side of the empty mesh and then take the needle back through the hole you came up. Just remember that you always return to the hole you came out of and always pick up a part of two stitches above. You will probably need more wool in your needle to cover the canvas properly. To fill in the little gaps that occurred when you skipped every other mesh at the beginning, work a little upright stitch or two to cover. The diagrams show how to add or subtract a stitch. This stitch has very little backing and will not bias the canvas.

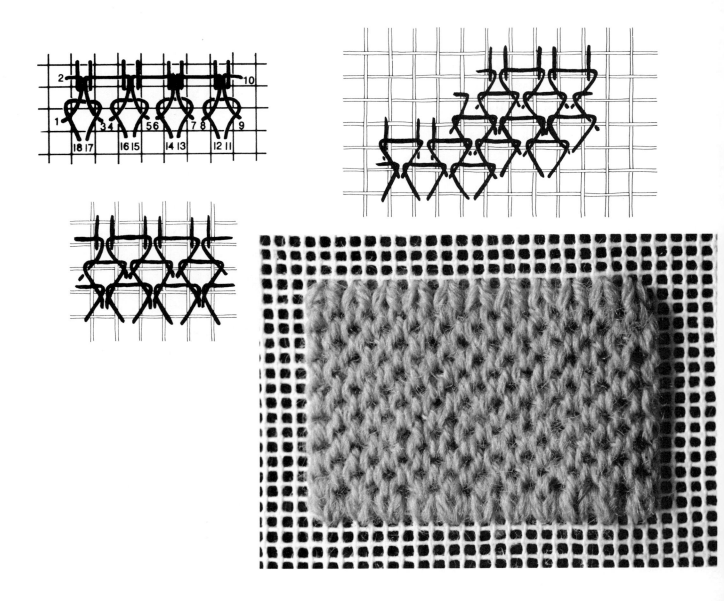

The Danish Knot Stitch

Both the Danish knot stitch and the French knot stitch were derived from straight embroidery. Perhaps the Danish version makes the transition to needlepoint a little better. It makes a more uniform knot and does not need a backgrounding of half cross stitch to cover the canvas as does the French version. In a border this stitch makes an unusual beading all by itself. Experiment with your wool until you achieve the size knot you desire. After taking the first stroke of the stitch (numbers 1 and 2) the rest of the stitch is worked on the face of the canvas until you finish at number 8.

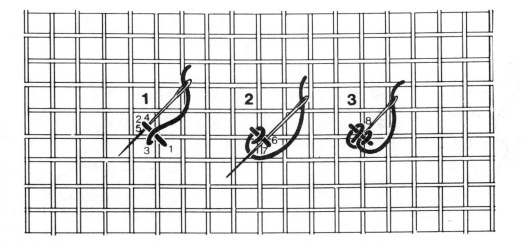

The Binding Stitch

The binding stitch is a finishing stitch and is important enough to deserve special mention. It is also known as the plaited edge stitch. It was originally used as a serging or covering for the selvages of one piece rugs. Now it is used as the decorative edging for glasses cases, bell pulls and tote bags as well as being used to join two pieces of canvas together. The stitch makes quite an enduring join as the wool passes through the canvas twice in the process of binding it together. The most important point to remember in the use of the binding stitch as a join is that the two pieces being joined must have an equal number of mesh to work over. The stitch forms a neat decorative braid which fits proportionately the canvas you are using. It is a reasonably malleable stitch in that it will turn corners and can be worked on a forty-five-degree angle.

Whether it is used as a join or by itself, it is worked over the folded edge of the canvas, using two mesh for mono-canvas and just one set of mesh for leno and the two-thread canvases. Fold the canvas back four or five mesh or sets of mesh right next to your finished needlepoint stitches. Hold the work with the wrong side facing you. The binding stitch has a slight tilt, and the tilt will be facing the right

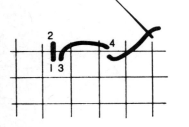
A

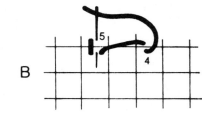
B

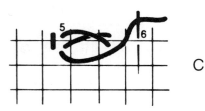
C

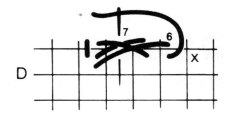
D

side if held wrong side towards you. You may need just a little less wool in your needle than you would for the half cross stitch on the same canvas. The stitch is always worked from left to right. Fasten the wool in the backs of nearby stitches and with the needle pointing towards you, take a few stitches in the first mesh to make a good cover for the beginning of the braid. Take the needle over the edge of the canvas to the third mesh, through that mesh and back over the edge of the canvas to the first mesh again. Yes, it is the same mesh where you worked all those beginning stitches. Now forward and over the edge again to the fourth hole, and back and over to the second hole, forward and over the edge to the fifth hole and then back and over to the third hole. You always skip a mesh going backwards, that is, you don't go into the very next mesh going back, but the mesh after that. You always go into the next empty mesh going forward.

When you come to a corner, just mitre it (see diagram) and sail on around the corner, going back and forth as usual just as if the corner were not there. When you come to the end of a thread of wool, finish it off on a forward stitch. Run the needle into the backs of nearby stitches to fasten it down. Start the new thread very near the old thread by running the needle up through the backs of completed stitches, bringing it up the very hole the old thread just completed, then go on with your stitching just as if it were the old thread. When you finish the area you want to cover, just stop working the stitch any further forward and work in place, so to speak, for a stitch or two so that the braid will have a completed look; weave the tag end of the thread up into the finished braid.

If you are joining two pieces of canvas with the binding stitch, they must have the exact same number of mesh on each side. Hold the two pieces wrong sides together and match mesh for mesh. Proceed with the stitch just as if it were only one piece. This stitch will not join two pieces of canvas flatly, for instance as a rug join, but if you wish to join two pieces or edges of a glasses case or purse in a knife edge, the stitch works beautifully.

Mitred Corner

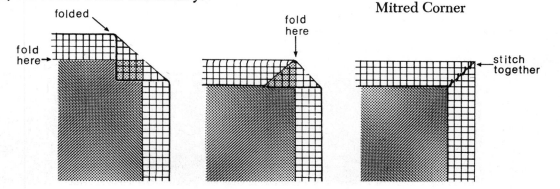

INDEX

110